OCCULT LINES BEHIND LIFE

M.P. PANDIT

LOTUS LIGHT

PO BOX 1008, LOTUS DRIVE
SILVER LAKE, WI 53170

Second U.S. edition April 24, 1992

Published by Lotus Light Publications by arrangement with Sri M.P. Pandit. Prior Indian editions published under the original title "Life Behind Life".

ISBN 0-941524-35-3
Library of Congress Catalog Card Number 79-63488

Printed in the United States of America

Printed on Recycled paper

SECTION ONE

OCCULT LINES BEHIND LIFE

CONTENTS:

The New Age

I have been frequently asked if there are any concrete signs by which one can know that the manifestation of a New Force, the Supramental Power, has really taken place, or whether it is a matter of faith. It is really a question which involves both, testimony and faith. At the present stage, faith is required at the outset. Testimony follows to corroborate. As things develop and the external results of the inner workings begin to emerge more clearly, faith or no faith, men will be obliged to recognise the presence of a new Factor, the Supramental Consciousness in action upon earth. As the Mother says, even the blindest will come to see.

"What testimony has come your way?" they ask. "Plenty," I would say. To speak in general terms, there has been a marked ascendency, during the last few years, of the forces working for harmony and peace over those that seek to wreck the progressive order of life. The possibility of a general war has been positively pushed back; a world war is most unlikely, more unlikely than ever, unless it comes as the bolt of Rudra to wipe out malignant remains of the old. Conflicts and clashes occur — rather, are allowed to occur — in the process of working out the collective Karma, but they are localised. It is unthinkable that a decade ago the Suez affair could have subsided in the manner it did. Or the Cuban crisis. Or, to come nearer home, the Chinese invasion. You may explain it in any way, but the fact remains that such a thing has not happened so far; it is something unique in history — I mean about their withdrawal.[1] Secondly, the

---

[1] This withdrawal of the Chinese, I am convinced, was first determined on the subtler planes. I know of an *upāsaka* who had the prevision and said — a month earlier — that the Chinese might just walk back. And we know they did.

realisation of Oneness among men and nations is stronger today than at any time before. It is penetrating more and more spheres of life. There is, further, an acute awareness among the leaders of thought that the human mind has reached the end of its tether and a further leap in evolution is indispensable if mankind is destined for a completer and happier life. There is a good deal of vigorous thinking on what is going to be the next step.

Most spectacular, however, are the results in the inner sphere, the spiritual. I have ascertained, and am in a position to state truthfully, that every serious spiritual seeker, whatever his path, finds a host of obstructions broken down. The barriers are removed. Those who meditate find it easier to collect themselves; those who pray proceed through the heart and find that there is an effortless intensity and keener aspiration in their seeking; those whose way lies through work find their dynamism quickened and their joy of consecration continuous. And for people in the Ashram it is a daily experience how the Mother's spiritual Force is today able to exact response from the most physical strata of life to a degree that was unknown before. Masses of illumination break upon cultivated and receptive minds, throwing open fresh vistas of possibilities. The human mind has been preparing itself for this hour and all over the globe there has been an air of expectancy as evidenced in the innumerable movements, collective and individual, that have been working and waiting for a New Age which they all feel and know is coming or has already come. The frames differ, the terminologies differ, but the central feature is the same: the old order is changing and a New Order is replacing it. Individuals, separated by thousands of miles of physical distance and many more of mental, are one in sensing and perceiving the outbreak of a New Agency — some call it Light, some Deity, others Faculty — in the Earth atmosphere. Almost all the traditions in the world have converged upon the present as the destined hour for the birth of the New Age, what Sri Aurobindo and the Mother have called THE HOUR OF GOD.

All this was forcibly brought home to me the other day when a leaflet found its way into my hands through the courtesy of a respected friend. It is issued by a group of seekers in Florida in the United States,[1] wedded to the Christian Faith and naturally using a language different from ours. Put in general terms, their faith and perception — and work based upon it — are this:

The Earth is now on the eve of entering into a Fourth Dimension. So long it has been the era of the expression of the material or Third Dimension on Earth. Various cycles — major and minor — are now coming to their climaxes. We are now in the final years of a "2,600 year cycle which is the revolution time of our Solar System around the Central Sun. Our planet Earth is also ending the 2,000 year cycle, called the Piscean Age. We are now in a final cleansing period, preparatory to the Golden Age. This is the long prophesied Harvest Period, the Age when all error must be swept from Earth and from the minds of those men who would remain for the millennium. For the Earth and all on it are even now in the process of being transmuted — raised to a higher vibration. We are now entering the Fourth Dimension, where all that exists on Earth, and the Earth itself, will exist in a higher state of evolution. There will be, and even now are in process, many changes in all forms of life. It is a natural step in the evolutionary progress of a planet, and will take place regardless of life existing on it. The many and varied Earth-changes already in effect, as well as the weather patterns and other related phases, are but small examples of how the entire Earth is to be changed for this Aquarian Age. This is not the end of the world, but the ending of an Old Age,

---

[1]Mark-Age, 327, 20 Terrace, Miami 37.

the cleansing of the old orders, so that the New Aquarian Age, in all of its spiritual glory, can occur."

The seekers in Florida go on to describe how vast changes are taking place everywhere and even body-structures are being affected. New vibrations are astir and the body of man, physical and mental, is responding variously. The Fourth Dimension is essentially a God-awareness, a state of Evolution where the 'Light of Truth' is patent, and there is an incessant pressure upon man to awaken and exercise his latent psychic and spiritual powers. "The Earth is being prepared to house a Race of a more highly developed and dedicated Man." There have come on Earth, adds the note, a large number of beings from other planets — some of them for the first time in 'fleshy bodies' — to take part in this great endeavour. The gigantic work is now in its final phase of the Preparation Period. "By 1965 there will be such a vast change in the thinking and in the desires of every man on Earth that it will be difficult for anyone to recall the turmoil and confusion which now exist here in every realm of life."

We are in substantial agreement with much that is said in this document of unusual depth. We may not be so definitive regarding the time-factor; our conception of the New Age and the New Race may be more far-reaching; but our experience and our vision are in the same direction.

The work is on. The question before everybody is what the Mother asks:

ARE YOU READY?

The Gods and Our Sadhana

Recently a prominent organiser of one of the Sri Aurobindo Study Circles put me a question. Is it permissible for the disciples of Sri Aurobindo and the Mother, who have taken up the Integral Yoga, to worship the traditional deities like Durga, Krishna, etc.? Can these celebrations be held in the Study Circle Meetings? At the moment I answered briefly that while the ritual of the worship of family deities could be carried on in the households as part of the social conventions by those who live as members of society, it was out of the question to bring in these activities at the meetings of the Circles which are expressly founded for the purpose of study and promotion of the Ideal and Yoga of Sri Aurobindo. Any proceedings which are not directly connected with the understanding and the practice of the Teaching of Sri Aurobindo and the Mother stand outside the legitimate scope of the Circle or the Centre.

Later I was asked to explain the position to a group of devotees and disciples to whom the question had posed some problems of understanding and adjustment. Why is it not possible to realise the New Ideal through the worship of the time-hallowed deities? Can they not give what we seek? Are they not Divine? It is quite natural to be perplexed in view of the facile generalisations to which men are accustomed, expecially in matters of this kind. It is commonplace now-a-days to hear, for instance, that all gods are one and it does not matter whom you worship. Learned people even take the trouble to quote a passage or two from the Veda to emphasise the point and repeat 'The one Existent the wise call by

different names'. We should all be catholic, respect each
other's beliefs, each other's gods, for ultimately we know all
are one. Of course, there are some who would smile
indulgently even at the mention of the gods. The gods are
concessions to the popular mind. Actually, they would say,
there are no gods or goddesses; they are just conceptual
crutches.

To start with the last point first. The Supreme Divine is
indeed something Absolute, Infinite, Ineffable. It is a sheer
Existence beyond any determination by Name and Form.
But that is not the whole truth. In this Existence all Name
and Form are implicit. And when the Divine moves into
manifestation, Form becomes inevitable. Nor is there any
possibility of an active relation between the Supreme
Existence and the manifestation without the mediacy of
Form. What relation can I, an individual in this manifestation, have with an Infinite for purposes of my life? Can I pray
to a featureless Peace, to an Ineffable Bliss? Besides, for the
workings of the manifestation also, some kind of formulation,
some particularisation is necessary. There is, for instance,
electricity all over. But that cannot be put to any use as it is. It
has to be channelled and centred somewhere in order that the
power of electricity may function for a purpose. Similar is the
need everywhere. For the working out of the Purpose of
manifestation, the Divine puts out different concentrations of
its Consciousness into the Creation. As the manifestation
unrolls itself, as newer and newer truths come to be
manifested, new Emanations are put forth with the appropriate charges. These are the Gods who are so many Powers and
Personalities of the Divine charged with definite functions in
the building and maintenance of the Cosmos. Known under
various names to man, they lend themselves to relation with
him. The Gods have a world of their own, their own
gradation and their respective fields of activity. They have
forms, but the forms are not fixed in our sense. The forms vary

in details according as the human consciousness that transcribes them varies from people to people. Apart from these Gods who are typal beings standing outside the evolutionary movement, there are occasional direct manifestations of the Divine for special purposes, the *Avatār*. The Avatar comes to participate in and help to lift up the evolving creation to a higher status and to establish a new Truth each time. Thus whether it is the Gods or the Avatars, they represent in Creation the special formulation of the manifesting Truth that they embody. They have actualised their truths in Creation and they are helping each individual to actualise them in himself. Each of them has it in his power to manifest and help manifest a particular aspect or poise of the Truth with which he is charged either singly or in association with other Gods. If I resort to a certain Deity it can give me what it carries within itself, and only that in a full measure. No doubt the Deity derives from the Supreme and is that Divine in its essence, but on that account it cannot function in the infinitude of the Divine; it is bound to the terms of its becoming; it is a part of an organised Creation. That is why when the Rishi in the Veda aspires to a large widening of his consciousness, he prays to Varuna; when he seeks wholeness of health in body, mind and life, he calls upon the Ashwins or Rudra to come to his succour; when he needs to build up a strong flame of aspiration, an irresistible will to break through the walls of Ignorance, he invokes Agni. The Rishi knows very well that all these Gods are but forms of the One. But he knows too that the Gods are manifestations of specific divine Energies and hence he calls only those who are relevant to his purpose at the moment.

I should know that if I pray to Hanuman, the God of life-strength, I can hope to get life-energy but not any other gift which is in the keeping of some other God. Similarly, if I pray to Rama or Krishna, at best I can receive the full realisation of the special Truth of the Divine which they came to manifest and establish. Each Deity is a canalised expression of a movement of the Divine Truth-Consciousness. And if I seek to realise in myself any Truth, I should approach and wait upon that Centre in the Cosmos which is charged with its expression. If today I want to achieve siddhi in the supramentalisation of my being and in its transformation, I have perforce to appeal to the Power, the Shakti, that is active for that purpose in the Person of Sri Aurobindo and the Mother. No other agency, past or present, can give that to me. This is to be borne in mind by those who tend to an over-simplification of things by saying that the Divine is everywhere and so everything can be had everywhere; in effect it comes to nowhere.

If any God or Avatar could do anything and everything then there would be no need to have so many Gods and Avatars. It is precisely because each one is empowered to manifest a particular truth and has his field fixed for him, that when another truth needs to be manifested, it is another Power or Personality that descends for that purpose. Someone said that Sri Krishna and Sri Aurobindo are the same and so Sri Krishna can give the fruit of Integral Yoga. Now, it is commonsense that, unless the Truth Sri Aurobindo represents is something more than what Sri Krishna brought into manifestation, there was no need for Sri Krishna to come again as Sri Aurobindo (assuming that both are the same — they are not quite that, but this is another subject). Sri Krishna came down to establish the Truth of the Overmental Consciousness on Earth. Centuries after, when the human consciousness has evolved further and registered higher developments and the time has arrived for a still greater Truth to manifest, the Truth of the Supramental, another Avatar in the form of Sri Aurobindo has had to come. He or His Shakti can alone give what He represents; not necessarily through their physical form but always through their essential, spiritual Personality. Neither the Divine nor the

Creation which is His expression is a monotone. The Truth is multitudinous and Its manifestation is equally many-sided, graded in the tiers of its becoming. Consequently graded and varied are the realisations of the Truth possible to the human consciousness; graded and varied too are the means therefor.

I have put things rather trenchantly for purposes of clarity. Actually there is considerable flexibility in the dynamics of manifestation and this applies to the workings of the Gods as well. There is, up to a point, a mutuality or interchange of functions among certain Deities but that does not abrogate the unique nature and purpose of each centrally. And even the mutuality or interchange takes place within the level upon which those Deities function. One level cannot do duty for quite another grade.

Even if transformation and supramentalisation cannot be secured through the offices of Rama, Sita, Krishna or Hanuman, is it not possible to pass through the aid of these gods to the kingdom of the supramental? This was the next question. I can only answer in the perspective of the seers of the Veda and the Upanishad that not all the gods are happy to let you pass beyond them. The Rig Veda describes in more places than one how the advancing Rishi is held up in his path by one god or another. The Upanishad observes how the gods are anxious that men should not come to know too much. Theoretically it is of course possible that by the force of one's sincerity and will one can pass through the doors of one realisation into another, but that implies an unusual strength and self-reliance on the part of the practitioner. A benevolent deity may also help in the journey; it depends upon so many factors. These are exceptional cases and cannot be made the rule.

Then what about the general public? was the last question. People are used to worshipping their traditional gods and they cannot be suddenly asked to discard them and take to new objects of worship. They have to be led through the means they are familiar with in the hope of their changing over gradually, as a result of either their own experience or slow pressure of Thought.

It is better to be frank on this point. The Yoga of Sri Aurobindo and the Object it sets for itself are not meant for the masses. Its effect on the generality can only be indirect. It is only a few who are prepared, or ready to be prepared, in some way or other, by previous evolution, that can hope to take the leap that is implicit in this Yoga. It is neither necessary nor useful to make propaganda and get adherence to this Teaching. The Circles are not centres for recruitment. Has not Sri Aurobindo categorically said that he does not believe in bringing the Truth to another's door? Those who have the seeking but find the existing means inadequate to meet their need, those who feel that the present religions, their rituals, the existing ideals have ceased to be a living power today, are bound to turn to newer and expanding affirmations of Truth and the means thereto. Publicity must be confined to making known the Ideal, the way to realise it as also the practical results achieved so far of effort in this direction. This is the function of the Centres and the Circles; to make known, to provide facilities for the understanding and the practice of the Yoga perfected by Sri Aurobindo and the Mother to achieve the Ideal of transformation of the human into a divine life. Even one single life earnestly dedicated to this Path and holding the Mother's Light in the heart with humility and good-will is sufficient to give meaning to each Centre, a candle to light other candles.

Naturally all this applies only to those who seek to practise the central Teaching of Sri Aurobindo and the Mother — their Yoga of Life Divine. There are other aspects which touch humanity at different levels — social, political, ethical, cultural, etc., and any one can profit by them without necessarily breaking with his past habits and the present grooves of convention.

Man and Animal Birth

I have often wondered what is the element of truth in the innumerable Puranic legends about men being cast back into animal births either as a result of their own Karma or because of some curse of an enraged god or Rishi. For we can be sure that behind all that is said and described in the ancient Puranas there is some core of truth somewhere, whatever may be the hyperbole or the embellishment indulged in to appeal to the popular mind.

Thus it is said that a royal sage Bharata, in spite of all the religious merit he had acquired, had to be born a deer for the simple reason that he came to conceive an inordinate attachment to a deer which he brought up as a foundling. A prince of the house of Sudas was, for no fault of his own, cursed by Vasishtha to be born as an ogre eating human flesh. The curse was undeserved and it acted as a boomerang inasmuch as the man so condemned took his revenge by neatly eating up all the hundred sons of the sage. That is, however, another story. Now is it really possible for a being, a soul, who has arrived at the human level in Creation to go back, to regress in the scale of natural evolution? Or are all these accounts simply didactic stories to instil fear into credulous minds and keep men to the righteous path?

We are assured on good authority that the normal line of soul-development is upward. A soul that has once reached the human stage does not go back to a lower level, curse or no curse. It is after a series of countless births — over eighty lakhs, say the Tantras — that the soul is brought up to the human gradation and it is inconceivable that the economy of Nature could permit a sudden turn-back, a retrogression after such an aeonic labour. But Nature is vast and elastic in her operations and we cannot bind her to too rigid a logical course either. There may be deviations under exceptional conditions.

Sri Aurobindo concedes one or two possible conditions under which a human soul may take an animal birth. Discussing the question, he points out that for a soul in the animal order to make a transition to the human, means a conversion of consciousness, a conversion radical enough to enable it to inhabit a human tenement and answer to the demands of Nature at that level. Now it may happen that in some cases the conversion of consciousness has not been deep enough and the being, after a tentative probing embodiment in the human organism, may find that its conversion is not as complete as required to give it the needed security of tenure under the new conditions. In that case it may go back to its old habitat to perfect its change and qualify fully for a secure human assumption.

Another likely condition is when the being has certain strong animal propensities which stick to it even after leaving the body and will not be shed in the normal course. They demand a satisfaction of fulfilment in their own kind and it is under such circumstances that the soul or, more correctly, a part of its vital personality attaches itself to a proper animal form and exhausts itself. Thus one with excessive greed for food may cling to a pig, one with inordinate sexual desire to a goat, one with a strong streak of unsatiated cruelty to a hyena, and so on. In all cases there is a loose holding of the animal body by the soul or part of it, till the karma is worked out and the soul freed to proceed on its way to the place of rest.

Barring such cases, we do not envisage the possibility of a human soul being relegated to the animal birth in the normal course. So far it is entirely rational and satisfying to my intelligence. But there is another class of phenomena which has intrigued me.

And that is the tradition that Mahapurushas, highly evolved or even perfected beings, choose to take animal forms and roam on the earth. This is not just an old wives' tale. There is unimpeachable testimony to these happenings even in our modern age. No less an exalted spiritual figure than Sri Ramana Maharshi has testified to this fact more than once. During the days when he lived in the caves on the hills of Arunachala — long before the present Ashram was formed — wild beasts like tigers and leopards, untamed creatures like serpents and mongooses, were regular frequenters of that region. And if human visitors would take fright and seek to harm them, the Maharshi used to ask them to desist, saying that the beasts would do no harm if only they were left alone. And besides, he added significantly, there were many Siddha Purushas living on the hills who came to see him assuming those forms.

Or to take yet another instance. In his interesting biography of Yogiraj Gambhirnath, a remarkable Natha Yogi who closed his earthly career in 1917, Prof. Akshaya Kumar Banerjea — a knowledgeable writer with a keen philosophical mind — records in connection with animals one notable incident narrated by the Yogi long after it had taken place.

"The Yogiraj incidentally mentioned that they were not always ferocious creatures, but that sometimes saints with extraordinary yogic powers moved on earth in the shape of serpents, tigers, etc. Different saints might have different reasons for assuming such bodies, but it was a fact that they did so. He referred to an event which he experienced on the bank of the Narmada. In the course of his journey in that region one particular spot attracted him. He found an empty cottage there. He entered it and was absorbed in meditation. The next morning a big serpent of extraordinary nature appeared before him, fixed its gaze upon him for some time, and then respectfully crept round him and went away. The sight of the serpent produced an inexplicable spiritual effect upon his mind and he passed into the state of trance. The second morning also the same serpent appeared and behaved in the same way and he obtained the same experience. This was repeated on the third morning as well. On that day a Brahmachari arrived and told him that he was the permanent occupant of the cottage. Of course he was not displeased with him for his occupying the cottage in his absence. In the course of conversation the Brahmachari informed him that an extraordinary Mahatma with spiritual attainments of a supremely high order was residing in that locality in the body of a serpent and that the Brahmachari had been dwelling in that cottage for twelve years in a prayerful and meditative mood with a view to having a darshan of the Mahatma!

"The Yogiraj told the disciples that this was not an exceptional incident and that there were many such Mahatmas dwelling in subhuman forms voluntarily or compulsorily for various reasons. He came across many such Mahatmas. He referred to his meeting some yogis living and moving in the guise of tigers."

Many questions arise.

In the first place, could all these things be really possible? I asked this to the Mother. The Mother says they are quite possible. Possibility conceded, what are the impelling factors, reasons 'voluntary or compulsory'? Why should beings, who have reached the top of the human evolutionary ladder and are freed from all moorings in the lower Nature, choose or be chosen to take subhuman embodiments? Could it be that only so it is possible to effect radical changes in those orders of animal creation? Just as the Divine comes down or sends His emanations in human form to work out crucial turns in the evolutionary progression of man, are animal embodiments similarly chosen to consciously work out similar difficulties and effect in the animal life changes necessitated by the general advance in Evolutionary Nature? Or could it be that certain developed beings are entrusted with different kingdoms in the animal creation? I do not know.

Good People and Suffering

It was only two days ago that I was narrating to my sister the terrible encounters and trials which Milarepa — the master Yogi of Tibet — had to face during his practice of Yoga. She exclaimed: "Why is it that suffering is always the lot of good people?" A good man, a god-fearing person has never a smooth life. One after another he receives checks and blows, whereas the bad ones prosper; even if they commit the very wrongs for which the good are penalised, God lets them go scot free. The plums of life go to the bad while the good groan. Why is that so in God's creation?

This in substance is the conundrum that has faced, time and again, many of those who think: If this world is really a creation of the Divine, why does the best in life go invariably to the least deserving? Not merely in the case of individuals, but even on a collective scale the question applies. Power and wealth flow more into wrong places while good and progress-ive causes languish for want of means. Such a state of affairs would seem to indicate that this world is not God's creation but the Devil's. Or perhaps the Illusionist is right after all in stigmatising the universe as a fantasy of Maya, a gigantic falsehood?

A closer consideration of the problem, however, reveals that this state of things — real enough to justify the accusing finger of the defeatist — is but natural in the present condition of our universe. I say *present* because the conditions in which Life functions in our cosmos are not fixed once for all; they are not permanently set. The world moves, *jagati*, and the conditions too move and change. Ours is an evolving creation, moving from one state to another, from lower states of consciousness to progressively higher and higher states, from Ignorance to Knowledge, from Darkness to Light. Our creation has evolved far above its original physical base in Inconscience but it is still in the realm of Ignorance and of its issue, Falsehood. The cosmic organisation as a whole still functions in the grip of the dark forces; all movements and velleities turn in their grooves. Everything is geared to serve the Powers that rule. All is naturally weighted in favour of Falsehood and what promotes it. This reign of the Asura will end only when it is replaced by the reign of the Deva. That is why every step in the direction of the growth of Knowledge and Light is vehemently opposed by the occupying powers of Ignorance. They are all marshalled to attack and smother every movement for liberation from their hold, whether individual or collective.

In this setting it will be clear why those that serve the empire of Ignorance find their way easier and inviting, while those that seek to affirm the claim of the True and the Right find themselves opposed at every step. All power now naturally vests in the Adversary and it will be so till it is fully wrested by the Divine. Only when that is done will the order of things change.[1] And this change is on its way. The struggle between the elements of Falsehood and Truth, of Darkness and Light, has been a constant feature of this creation from its birth but each decisive battle has been won by the progressive Forces of Light. The war is still on but it is now in the last phase, and with the plenary emergence of the direct Consciousness-Force of the Divine — what we call the Supramental Power — the victory of the Divine is certain. The balance of forces is already showing signs of change. The long-established order of things is gradually yielding place at some levels to the pressure of the New.

Relevant to the subject is a legend in Teutonic mythology which is very significant. In this tradition, Valhalla is the

---

[1] The individual aspect of the question has been discussed elsewhere.

heavenly paradise of Heroes who die in battle and win a place in the community of gods. The whole day they engage themselves in fierce fighting and retire by the evening. During the nights, their wounds heal up and they feast together till dawn when the fighting is resumed. Now, the gods once realised that they needed to have a strong castle for their dwelling as it was not always convenient to be on the back of fluffy clouds. A mighty big castle, in keeping with their exalted status, was required and they approached the burly titans and asked for their help in the construction of the edifice. The titans agreed but on one condition and that was this: after the castle was ready the gods were to part with one of their goddesses — the goddess of LOVE. The gods were in a quandary. They took counsel among themselves and one of them, a hopeful, suggested that the construction would take long years, at the end of which they could see how things shaped. In the meanwhile they could assent. And so, hoping that something would intervene in their favour later on, the gods accepted the proposal.

The titans set to work. They piled up mountains after mountains and with surprising speed they completed the job. A magnificent castle was ready. Now it was the turn of the gods to fulfill their part of the bargain. Nervously they broached the subject to their goddesses and great was the wail sent up by the goddesses. The titans demanded their due; the goddesses would not agree. There was an *impasse*. Then one god, a wise one, spoke to the assembly of titans persuasively and pointed out how impractical it would be for so many giants like them to have only one goddess. Would it not be more welcome to all of them, he proceeded, to have immense gold instead that would suffice for everybody? The titans fell in, but insisted that the quantity of gold must be so much as would cover up entirely the figure of the goddess of Love from top to toe, from side to side, so that not a part of her could be seen. *Gold shall put away from sight the very visage of*

LOVE.

All available gold was collected from everywhere, from everyone, by the gods and it was heaped up all around the goddess of Love. And when this was done the titans were called in to take their due. Gleefully they trooped into the hall where the ceremony was held and as they looked closely at the gold-wrapped figure, they found that one small lock of her golden hair was hanging out through a small chink in the heap.

"No, no," they said, "we will not accept this gold. This crevice too shall be filled up." The gods were in consternation; for every bit of gold in heaven had been combed up and nothing was left with any goddess. They found that the only gold that remained was the gold ring on the finger of Wotan, the King of the gods. But how could Wotan the King part with his ring? For it was the ring of authority, the sceptre that conferred and affirmed his lordship over all and, if he were to part with it, he would have to part with his kingly power too. The gods were in a fix: Love or Power? They deliberated and ultimately decided in favour of keeping Love and entreated their king to give the ring which alone could cover up the crevice and save the goddess of Love for them. Reluctantly Wotan agreed. But before parting with the ring of Power, he held it in his palm and cursed it saying that whoever wore the ring of Power would go corrupt and perish.

The chink was duly filled up. The titans rejoiced in their gain of Power and Gold. The gods were content with the goddess of Love.

And to this day it has been so. All Power — Power that corrupts — and all Gold, *i.e.,* wealth, vest in the hands of the Adversary. But the gods have in their possession Something which is greater than all power, all wealth — the Truth of Love in whose alchemy the very texture of life is slowly changing.

Ill-Will

"Don't speak of your troubles to others," advises a retired Admiral, who has had, evidently, a good bit of experience. For, he says, "Half the people to whom you speak do not really care what happens to you; and the other half are d—d glad of it!" And I would add, the same advice would hold good when things go well with you. Do not speak of it to others.

It was some time last year. I was in a fairly bright period and happened to meet a friend who was passing along. We exchanged greetings and then he asked me how I was getting on. I told him I was fine. He enquired in detail, of my health, my work, my studies and I was naturally very enthusiastic in my answers. "That means you are happy", he observed laughingly and we parted. And from that moment I ceased to be happy. Things started going wrong; irritations galore; I developed a cold and signs of 'flu. I did not at first understand the reason for this sudden turn of events. Slowly it dawned on me and I hastened to inform the Mother. Needless to say, I became all right very soon and was told by Her, a little later, to be quiet and not to speak of what goes on.

This is not a solitary instance of the kind. We all know how often things take an unexpected turn when particular persons happen to see or take note of them. My sister tells me how, if certain people pass by at the time when flavouring ingredients are being added to the dishes under cooking, the fragrance dies completely. Whole plants wither away once they strike some people with their luxuriant growth. Jack fruits fall from the tree the moment some passer-by admires them and passes a remark on the fortune of their owner. Cows giving plentiful milk go dry for no apparent reason. A child is

dressed up and sent on promenade; some one sees and remarks, "How beautiful!"; the same night it gets ill. An infant
is unusually quiet and does not cry often. A neighbour or
visitor expresses surprise, and nine times out of ten, the child
starts crying. And so on.

I have often wondered at the cause of such phenomena
and the other day I asked the Mother about it. The Mother
said that the causes are many and vary from case to case.
Broadly they can be placed under two categories: human and
non-human. But in either case the bad-will of individuals is
the instrumentation.

Coming to the first type: there are men who are so made
by nature that they cannot bear to see the well-being of
others. Be it noted that their own conditions of affluence or
indigence does not at all count in these matters. When they
come across anybody or anything which is in a good,
prosperous state, their ill-will is aroused and it emits
vibrations that attack the object of their resentment. It is not
that they are always conscious. Very often the individual is
not aware of his real reactions below the cultivated surface of
his being; the movement of jealousy and bad-will is there
somewhere in the subconscious. But as far as the poor victim
is concerned, it is all the same; the results are equally concrete
in either case. It is also likely that the person from whom the
adverse current emanates is normally a good person; all of a
sudden something rises up from his nature and strikes out at
that moment.

We say that good-will, benedictions, kind thoughts have
a beneficial effect. So too with things of the other kind. One
cannot be too careful against such attentions. The best way is
not to attract too much notice but to be quietly happy with
gratitude to the Divine for keeping one in that state of well-
being.

Not all such set-backs, however, are due to others. There
are individuals who are prone to too much imagination,

nervous by temperament and they go on anticipating attacks with the result that certain mental formations get crystallised in their atmosphere and produce the apprehended results.

Then there are causes of the other kind: forces, entities, beings in the subtler world that are always on the look-out for openings to break, to confuse and if possible to destroy. The Mother has pointed out how when some people jubilantly announce the end of their troubles — maybe of health, maybe of any other type — there is an immediate slide-back and the trouble starts all over again. That is because the hostiles are provoked into activity, they take it as a challenge and go all out to undo what has been the occasion for the rejoicing. Do not be too loud, warns the Mother. They may move into action directly or through human individuals whose proverbial bad-will is ever at their disposal. Any movement of joy and happiness, any development in the direction of progress, opulence, perfection acts as a bull's-eye to these cohorts of the Adversary who are akin to the

"Ominous beings...

Whose very gaze was a calamity."

(Sri Aurobindo: *Savitri*)

On Matters Physical (I)

It is always an education to listen to Medhananda.[1] Whether he talks to you on a serious subject or makes a remark in passing on a casual topic, there is always something new, a different look which throws a fresh light on the matter. Carrying in himself the true spirit of two civilisations, one the Western as developed in its finest strains in Europe, and the other an ancient way of life in the bosom of Mother Nature under the unveiled firmaments of the Spirit as come down in the peoples of the Pacific, he represents the best of at least two traditions. I say *at least* because I feel in him the breath of more. Judged by the facility with which he gets into the spirit of earlier civilisations like the Egyptian, Greek etc. and the spark he communicates to you, I have no doubt he has lived them most intimately in his past lives. What is more surprising is that even among things Indian he strikes depths that are missed by many of us.

He is a man of wide interests. His discerning intelligence[2] uncovers the grain, doing away with the chaff, with a facility that is astonishing. He has feeling for the Lone Spirit of Shankara, he has attraction for the countenance of Peace in the face of the Buddha, he has eyes for the dark beauty of an unusual Parvati in bronze, he has the perception that gets at the lore of Wisdom which lurks behind Grimm's Fairy Tales. Small happenings, turns of phrase, gesture, action or reaction in every-day-life throw him into moods that land him into the Life behind life. But by no means is he moody.

[1]The versatile Librarian at our Sri Aurobindo International Education Centre. The pre-ashram name of this one-time Judge in Germany is Fritz Winkelströter.

[2]Like all names given by the Mother, the name chosen for him is particularly apposite: *Medhānanda*, one whose nature delights in the scintillations of the intellect.

Quick to perceive what is wrong, he discovers at the same moment why it is wrong and supplies the corrective with an equal ease.

Recently we had a visit by a coach from Europe to train our girls in the Olympic events. There was a demonstration. For the item of parallel-bars a bowl had been kept on the ground with magnesium oxide with which to rub the hands so as to keep them from slipping. Each of the participants bent down to help herself with the oxide. But there was a marked difference when the coach did it; it was a picture of grace when she swiftly bent down and stood up with the minimum of movement, in the minimum of time. No one seemed to notice it but it did set M. into a reminiscent mood. Decades ago, he told me, he had read somewhere about the Buddha a narrative which began with the line: *The Perfect One sat down without using his hands.* At the end, it concluded: *The Perfect One stood up without using his hands.* It made a deep impression on him at that time and it came up into his mind when he saw this lady doing things with the utmost economy of movement.

This is a thing, he says, that is sadly lacking in our youth. Grace in bearing, economy of movement of the physical body and a natural rhythm in the gait, which come so naturally to those in Europe who have gone through even the elementary stages of physical training, are yet to be acquired. Look at any boy or girl sitting on a chair reading a book. He is found spreading himself in a lackadaisical position, with legs either dangling loosely or in a perpetual movement without purpose. A piece of paper falls down. Look again how he picks it up. He bends sideways, stretches out one loose hand, gropes with the fingers, the leg goes up in a jerk; he does not succeed at once in picking up the object; another uncouth movement, and so on.

The whole proceeding offends an aesthetic eye. It jars on a sensitive spirit that looks for beauty in the creation of God.

As the Mother has pointed out repeatedly, the Divine manifests in the Physical, in the world of physical forms, primarily as Beauty — beauty of form, symmetry in proportion, harmony in movement. We see this to a certain extent in Nature below the human level. Man shall use his freedom and superior power to further this movement of expression of Beauty, and not go counter to the Intention in Nature. The Physical is a mould of the Divine to manifest its glory and it is incumbent upon us to cherish and promote all that raises its value, both as a base and an effective means, for this manifestation. The physical body, with the energy that flows through it, is a thing to be cherished and used to the utmost advantage. Not a movement, not a gesture shall be wasted. A body so disciplined grows not only into a vehicle of conserved power, but develops also a consciousness which makes it self-active. The limbs move spontaneously into action that reflects the mood of the soul — natural *mudrās* spoken of in our ancient treatises.

This brings me to the unfortunate twist given to the Indian tradition, sometime in the long course of its evolution, by which the Physical has come to be treated with utter negligence, if not with a positive contempt. I shall not go here into the reasons that led to this development. I shall only draw attention to the ruinous consequences of this deviation from the genius of the nation's soul. I do not need to point out that with the fathers of our civilisation in the present cycle, the Rishis of the Veda, Mother Earth had equal claims on man with Father Heaven. A full-limbed body living for full hundred summers, filling the skies with full-throated hallelujas to the glory of the commonwealth of gods and men, gathering in two hands the treasure of both the Matter and Spirit, *anna* and *rayi*, was their ideal. This continued till late into the age of the Upanishads when the attention began to be directed more and more exclusively to the Spirit to the detriment of Matter. The Ascetic, the Sannyasin who turned

away from the body of God in his passion for God, became
the ideal instead of the Rishi who laid down the law to hold
both the Earth and Heaven in a happy balance. The world
came to be looked upon as an illusion, as a snare to be escaped
from. All that belonged to the world, the Earth, was treated
as the enemy. The culmination of this movement was the
deliberate neglect, the abandonment, of the Physical —
which most embodies the principle of this Earth, *Pṛthivī* — to
its own fate and an extreme preoccupation with the Soul.
The springs of life dried up. And with the disuse and failure of
the life-energies, came the decline of our material civilisation.
We touched the nadir. Today things are changing, no doubt,
but the weight of the legacy is there. We still look upon the
Physical, and things pertaining to the physical, — physical
work for instance — as degrading. Recently there was a
report that at a national undertaking where technicians of a
German firm are helping, the disparity between the visiting
team and their Indian counterparts was so great that the
visitors wondered how at all the plant could be run on
economic lines by our men. It appears that man to man one
German was found equal to three Indians in the output of
work. When I mentioned this to M. he was not surprised, for,
as he explained, in the West, especially in a country like
Germany, they attach great value to manual work and the
national mind is trained to it. Working with the hand is as
important to them as working with the mind.[1] And this, he
added, was so in the past in the East also. In China, for
instance, a potter who designed and produced a novel
porcelain jar in a unique blue was made a Duke. In India too
there must have been an age when hand-work, concentration
upon the physical aspect with a view to drawing the best from

---

[1] We all know how the German race is as famous for its meticulous organisation of the
material side of life as for its thoroughness in the intellectual field. History has no parallel to
the gigantic effort made by them in successfully reconstructing their country within a decade
after the last war which had brought destruction on a total scale.

it, was respected. He could not imagine a race of men who looked down upon the physical side — work on and in the physical — producing the magnificent sculptures and architectural wonders which exact the admiration of the world even today.

His first shock in this regard, he told me, came during the first days of his stay in India. Some light statues had to be carried to the main Ashram building from the library. He could not do it alone by himself and requested an Indian colleague of his to assist. But the latter was horrified: "It is *his* work", he replied, pointing to a servant. My friend was taken aback. "And the statues were of Gods!" he exclaimed, perhaps in an oblique reference to our oft-vaunted claim for superiority as a 'spiritual people'.

It is a fact. We as a race have long lost touch with the Divinity in Matter. That is why we have developed a scale of values in which the Physical, the needs and claims of the material side of life, occupy the lowest rung.[1] But this has got to be corrected if we at all hope to move with the peoples of the world and take our due place as participants in the building up of a Humanity which shall be an ample figure of the Universal Godhead manifest in the highest terms of Harmony, Beauty, Peace and Joy.

The human brain, M. explains, has different areas devoted to the workings of different limbs of the body. Of these the portion related to the hand — one hand — is as big as the portion connected with both the legs. That shows the design in evolving Nature. Men have succeeded and established their supremacy over their environment and built up societies in the measure in which they have utilised the *hand*. The very word culture derives from the root *ku* which means

---

[1] Contrary to the common understanding, Medhananda does not concede that Spirit and Matter are high and low. They are, he explains, two ends of a pole. He prefers to cite the figure of a serpent whose tail is curled up and faces its mouth. The 'distance' between the two is illusory; the mouth touches the tail. Actually the two ends are nearer to each other than to any point in between.

to cultivate — dig with the hand, the hand signifying manual effort. It may be said that it is through the human hand that the Divine takes hold of Matter; the hand is the link between the gods and the physical world. (The word for hand in Latin, it may be noted, is *manus*.)

The value attached to physical work,'doing with the hands',was brought home to me one day in an unexpected manner. An engineer from the United States was on a visit to the Ashram. He was most highly qualified and I believe his income ran into four or five figures. In spirit with the life of the Ashram, he offered to do some work and took on an assignment. Imagine my surprise the next day to see him kneeling on the floor with a hammer and other instruments in his hands and going it all alone. I asked myself involuntarily if any Indian engineer would have worked like that, doing even the work of a 'mechanic'. My own mentality reflected something of this general attitude in our country. It is below our dignity to do manual work. Those who do it do so out of necessity, but all the while they feel that their work is 'inferior'. If some do it voluntarily — as say in public life — they are conscious all the time that they are doing something unusual and expect commendation for their condescension. No wonder we fail in the material field.

The truth of the matter is indeed self-evident. The Mind will respond and yield its secrets only when one cultivates it deliberately, puts oneself in its service and enlarges its field of expression in oneself. So with the soul, so with the source of vital energy. So too with the physical. Unless I respect the Purusha in matter and wait upon it with devotion, discipline and application, the physical will not yield its treasures to me.

Due attention to the domains of the material organisation of life is necessary to succeed in this world. But it is much more necessary, even indispensable, in a yoga like ours which includes the full utilisation and the transformation of the

Physical in its aims. The Physical is a field both for training and for expression in this Yoga. The Mother has emphasised again and again the value of physical work, the importance of the physical in the total development of man which is the meaning of our yoga. Without perfection at the base there can be no real perfection at the top. It is a mistake to look upon the mind or the heart as superior to the body. An essay in thinking, a poem of devotional ecstasy, a piece of physical work done in the right spirit are all equal in the eyes of the Divine. As She says, what makes a thing really important or unimportant is the spirit in which it is done, the consciousness that is put into it. Even if it be to sweep a room, put all thy attention and soul into it and make it as clean as a first-class operation theatre. Be thorough, be perfect, whatever the field in which thou art called upon to work.

All is Divine and all shall be treated as Divine, regarded in equal sacredness and waited upon and served in the highest measure of sincerity. The Physical is a concentrated expression, a meaningful formulation of the Divine. Respect the Divine in the Physical, organise its expression in and through thee with all the fervour and delicacy thou hast reserved for the Lord of thy being. He is not only on the heights, but waits for thy greeting in the depths as well.

On Matters Physical (II)

When the Mother speaks of Beauty as the characteristic form in which the Divine manifests in the Physical world, it is not only Beauty in Form that is meant but also Beauty in Movement. Beauty lies in symmetry, in harmony of proportions, true; but it lies equally in the movements of what is so built. Hence, for a seeker of the Integral Yoga which aims to realise the Divine in each of His manifestations, it is as much necessary to cultivate and express a feeling for beauty in Form — in himself and in others — as it is to shape and perfect beauty in his bodily movements. In a word, he must observe himself and take steps to eliminate all that is uncouth and offensive to the aesthetic sense in his physical dispositions and at the same time develop movements that are elegant, graceful and can faithfully express the growing evolution of his soul in outer mobile forms of harmony and beauty.

It is commonly ignored, but a truth nevertheless, that our physical movements have a significance beyond their material figuration. They are, in fact, a projection, a reflex on the physical level, of the working of the many forces that are active on the subtler planes of our being, e.g. our vital, our emotional being, our mind etc. Each physical movement is the culmination of a series of stresses that are not visible and hence a reflection, a live symbol of the totality of forces that precipitate themselves in that form. Reversely, if we consciously make a particular movement, it induces — whether intended or not — an action leading to the same play of forces that normally bring that movement into being. And that is, after all, the meaning of the *mudrā* so commonly used in the Tantras, or for that matter in the rituals of all religions. Specific gestures are made with hands and fingers and corresponding subtle movements are automatically set into motion. A *mudrā*, or gesture, of surrender made with full consciousness initiates a wave of self-giving; similarly, a *mudrā* of call, *āvāhana*, releases a vibration or a series of vibrations, which go forth to invoke the Deity that is waited upon. Thus the *mudrās*, when performed in the proper consciousness, function as channels of communication and agents for effectuation.

It is not that these *mudrās* have meaning only in matters of ritual where special factors are at work. Even in our normal day to day life, certain gestures, certain postures do set into motion particular activities of forces with the physical movement as their nodus. I remember having heard that Sri Ramakrishna once reproved someone (was it Naren?) for sitting with his cheek on the palm of his hand. This posture indicates some worry, some mental tribulation, and it can also call into action movements that result in mental unease. So also there are certain postures of sitting or lying down which act like a magnet to forces of tamas and inertia. Each physical movement, like each mental movement, has a meaning and significance and it behoves the seeker of the Integral Yoga to be very conscious in the matter and encourage only those movements that build up the forces of light, harmony and beauty. Those that are graceful, elegant and pleasing to the eye are indeed the elements that help to form the proper milieu for the manifestation of the Truth of Beauty, even as the opposite ones repel its advent.

I was reading the other day a remarkable book by a thirteenth-century administrator-scholar of Persia, Nasir-ad-Din Tusi written at the behest of his superior, the Governor of Quhistan. In spite of its title,[1] it is really a treatise on Practical Philosophy of perennial interest. He makes a number of observations in the section on the education and

[1] Nasirean Ethics.

regulation of children which seemed to be relevant to the line of thinking that started this causerie. No doubt his approach is not from the spiritual standpoint. But it is in the right direction with aesthetic overtones and can very well prepare for a more purposive discipline.

Thus speaking on *Manners of movement and rest*, he enjoins: "In walking one should not move quickly or in haste, for that is a sign of frivolity, nor, however, should one go to exaggerated lengths in dawdling and slowness, for that is a mark of sloth. One should not strut like the arrogant, or move the shoulders in the manner of women and effeminate men. The dangling and the movement of the hands are also to be guarded against, equilibrium being preserved in all situations. When walking, a man should not much look behind, for such is the action of loutish persons. Nor, however, must the head be held constantly forward, for this is an indication of grief and overwhelming anxiety. In riding, likewise, equilibrium is to be preserved. When sitting, the feet should not be put forward, nor should one be placed on the other. One should kneel only in subservience before kings, a master, a father, or anyone comparable to these persons. The head should not be rested on the knees or the hands, for that is a mark of grief or sloth. One should not hold the neck bent, nor play with the beard or other members. Let not the finger be placed in the mouth or the nose, and let not noise be produced with the fingers, the neck or the other members. Yawning and stretching are to be avoided. . . ."

On *eating*:

"First, hands and mouth and nose should be cleansed, and then one may appear at table. When one takes one's seat at table, one should not proceed to eat directly, unless one be the host. The hand and the clothing should not be soiled, not more than three fingers should be employed in eating, and the mouth should not be opened wide. The eater should not take up large morsels, nor should he swallow quickly or keep his mouth full. Let him not lick his fingers. At the same time, he should not inspect the different varieties of food, or sniff at them, or make a selection from them. If the best dish be scant in amount, let him not fall upon it greedily, but rather offer it to others. Grease should not be left on the fingers; bread and salt should not be made damp. One should not look at one's fellow-diners, nor inspect the morsels they take, but eat with one's face forwards. That which is taken to the mouth (we refer to such things as bones) should not (afterwards) be placed on the bread or the table-cover, when there is a bone or a hair in a morsel of food, let it be removed from the mouth in such a way that no one else is aware.

Let a man beware of committing that which he finds repulsive in others. . . .

A man should not withdraw his hand (from eating) some considerable time before the other guests; rather, if he feels himself satisfied, should he while away the time until the others also finish. If, however, the assembly as a whole withdraw their hands, he should do likewise, even though he be hungry; an exception may be made where he is in his own home or in a place where there are no strangers present. If, in the course of a meal he feels the need for water, let him not drink it hastily so as to produce noises from the mouth and gullet. . . . When he washes, he should not gargle or spit into the basin."

On *speech*:

"One should not speak much nor interrupt the speech of another by one's own. Whenever someone is relating a story or a tale of which one already has knowledge, one should not reveal one's knowledge thereof, so that the person in question may complete his discourse. Let no man answer to a matter that is asked of another. If a question be put to a group of which he is one, let him not try to outstrip the others. If some one be already occupied with making answer, and he be capable of giving a better, he should be patient until that answer is completed, then giving his own in such a way as to offer no affront to his precedent. Let him not plunge into any discussions being carried on by two persons in his presence; and if they should conceal their remarks from him, let him not try to overhear. . . . When dealing with his superiors a man should not speak in allusions, nor should he keep his voice high or low, but observe a mean. . . . When others are developing an argument before him, he should not take it upon himself to reply until the argument is complete. When he does speak, he should not make any pronouncement before first fixing the idea in his mind . . . in the course of his speech, let him not gesture with hands and eyes and eyebrows, unless what he is saying demands some delicate gesture, then he may perform it in the approved manner. . . .

Slander, calumny, false accusations and lying are to be avoided: indeed, in no circumstance may one engage therein. . . .

Listening should be practised more often than speaking: a wise man was asked why his listening exceeded his utterance, to which he replied: "Because I have been given two ears, but only one tongue — that is to say, you must listen twice as much as you speak!"

Asanas and Our Yoga

"Why is it that the yoga-asanas occupy a very minor place in your system of physical education? Why are Swedish exercises and the like given so much prominence? All over the country there is an awakening of interest in the efficacy of asanas and the governmental agencies are encouraging the starting of new centres for training in the asanas. But here, in an Ashram like this, they are relegated to the background. Why?"

It was an educationist earnestly speaking to me the other day. Just a couple of days earlier a team from a Yoga Institute in the North had asked me for our manual of asanas. On my telling them that we had no such treatise among our publications, they were frankly surprised and, to make sure that I had understood them aright, they asked me further what *kriyās* we did in the yoga here. It was not a new query. For, times without number visitors and correspondents — specially from the West — are intrigued when they find that asanas do not form part of our daily routine in the Ashram. And I understand their difficulty. Somehow a misunderstanding has grown up in the common mind that yoga means asanas or at any rate consists to a large extent of a schedule of asanas. Now, before touching upon this question of asanas in Yoga, let me first deal with the objection raised at the outset by the well-meaning friend.

It is not that asanas do not find a place in our system of physical education. Actually there is a separate section conducted by an expert in the line and it is being availed of by those who are particularly interested in it. But, by and large, the number of persons who participate in its activities is negligible. Asanas, it need not be explained, are special postures and movements of the body and its limbs made in order to derive certain benefits for physical growth and well-being. Properly done under suitable guidance, they build up and promote solidity, endurance and elasticity in the body. They regulate the circulation of the blood and direct it to the maximum advantage. They keep the whole system in a fine glow of health, free from ordinary diseases caused by congestion or obstruction in the normal functioning of the physiological apparatus. Beyond this they do not normally go. They do not directly build up strength; nor do they form the muscles. A well-directed programme of physical exercises should aim not only to keep the system in sound working condition, but to build up a muscular body with sufficient reserves of strength. It is not enough, moreover, to attend to the body *in situ*; the body in movement is also to be trained. If fuller attention is paid to the movements of the body in its various limbs and they are exercised intelligently, there grows an agility, a grace or beauty of movement. And if these individual movements are trained to synchronise with the movements of others on a collective scale, the body learns to move in a rhythm, to vibrate to a leading note as a conscious being. The body is taught to respond spontaneously and function as a conscious member. These are the governing principles of the rhythmic exercises popularised in the Scandinavian countries and adopted with much profit elsewhere too. Helpful aids like music, games, etc. are pressed into service and the whole movement is turned into a pleasant, interesting and at the same time highly beneficial exercise. The aim of the Physical Culture Training at our Educational Centre is not only to build up a strong physique, but also to develop its innate capacities of agility, rhythm, beauty and conscious self-direction. Only so could the body express to an extent the divine Truth of Beauty in Form which is its function to manifest in this Creation. Something of this was attempted with considerable success in the ancient communities of Greece. But it was not followed up in the succeeding civilisations.

It will be obvious why the system of asanas alone is totally inadequate for this purpose. Besides, our system does not consist of 'Swedish drill' alone, either. It represents a balanced combination of different systems of Physical Culture so as to develop the human body in all possible directions.

Then to come to the poser: why no asanas in our yoga?

Yoga means union, union with the Divine; by usage it also covers the means used for effecting that union. The means are several and so several are the yogas. Each of them has its own technique; each bases itself on any one power or one group of powers in the human system. One of the Yogas is Hatha Yoga which is organised around the physical body and the life-energy that vivifies that frame. This Yoga consists — to put it in general terms — of a series of bodily exercises, manipulation of the limbs, aimed at freeing the body from the normal limits imposed by Nature on its capacity of endurance, plasticity and longevity. These exercises or postures called *āsanas* are combined with certain breathing exercises known as *prāṇāyāma* (lit. lengthening of the life-breath) which establish a sure control on the course of the life-breath, purify the nerve channels and exert a stilling effect on the whole system. In result there is an intimate collaboration between the body and prana which leads to the third step, that of directing the concentrated life-force on to the basic centre of all Power in the body, lying practically untapped in the "subtle sheath" at a point corresponding in the "gross sheath" to the base of the spinal column. This centre, when so struck and awakened, releases a dynamic power, Kundalini, the central Shakti of which all energies in the body are secondary formulations. This Power rises upward through the various levels of our being, governed by different *tattvas* or principles — the physical, the vital, the emotional, the mental, etc. — till it reaches the centre at the top of the head where vibrates the plenary Divine Consciousness. Once the Shakti joins this Consciousness at the summit, there is a downpour of bliss bathing the whole system in the bliss of union, *yoga*.

This in main is the course of Hatha Yoga. It starts with the asanas which yield spectacular results in the body, overcoming the normal laws of nature, and that is what most appeals to the popular imagination. To the common man, both in the East and the West, yoga has consequently come to mean this discipline of asanas which gives control over the body, builds up an uncommon endurance, increases longevity and, when combined with pranayama, gives also a control over certain types of subtle phenomena which strike the eye with their miraculous impact.

But the asanas have only a preliminary, enabling role. Even in Hatha Yoga they are not the whole of it. They build only the first, the basic part of the edifice. In Raja Yoga where also they are used, they play a secondary role, the main process being psychological purification and control of the internal organ of the mind in all its complexity. Asanas are used to support and promote this control and purification. In other yogas — the Bhakti, Karma, Shabda, Laya Yoga, etc. — the asanas may not be used at all. In our yoga also there is no necessity to adopt all the laborious and time-taking methods of asana or pranayama. What is sought to be achieved by asanas in the yogas where they are commonly resorted to, is here done by methods other than physical or physiological. Psychological and psycho-spiritual means like meditation, concentration, prayer, inner surrender are adopted.

In Hatha Yoga the body is controlled, collected and its movements so directed as to exert a pressure on the mind and on the other deeper and higher centres of power in the system. The physical energies are stilled; the life-energies are purified and both are directed to awaken the hidden centres of spiritual power. In Raja Yoga the mental energies are similarly controlled, purified and made to exert their pressure upward so as to open up the region just above the mind. It proceeds from below upwards. In this yoga the movement is more natural: it is from above to below, from the higher to the lower. It is the higher spiritual Consciousness and Power that are invoked directly from the heart or by concentration in the head and that are directed on the lower members like the mind, the life, the body, so as to calm them, purify them and uplift them to their own higher nature. Thus the restlessness of the mind and the impetuosity of the life-force are stilled in the Peace that descends from above or spreads out from within. That way, the effort is much less strenuous and the results more secure.

This is the normal course in our yoga. Asanas are not necessary, much less indispensable. As for those who need or prefer to utilise aids like asanas or pranayama for their yogic progress, they are certainly free to do so. Asanas are not enjoined upon anyone; but they are not prohibited, either. They can be utilised if they are found useful and as long as they are found necessary.

Mind Control

Someone has classified men into two categories: the race-horse type and the farm-horse type. Those who come in the first are habitually high strung, living at great speed, wearing themselves out in no time. Those that belong to the second are slow, leisurely in movement and generally easy-going. Most of us would have no difficulty in saying which label fits us. At any rate I instantly recognised myself as the race-horse type. For I have always been of the kind that lives at a high pitch. Even when there is no need to be hurried and there is plenty of time to do things, I must go at it in a spirit of now or never. The nerves are tense; the brain is intent and the mind cannot make room for anything else till the thing is done. And even when it is over, there is no stopping. "What next? What next?" The system is in a continual state of tension, excitement and rush. And I had always thought that this was the only right way to act. It had never occurred to me that things could be done otherwise. My eyes opened only when I saw the Mother at work. I observed that the Mother would not be stampeded even in the midst of the most pressing urgencies. The very air about Her would be so quiet as to appear almost remote from 'reality'. She takes up each item — whether it is reading or writing or doing anything — in a measured, controlled manner and proceeds as if the whole of eternity is there to complete the job. It is a picture of calm collected power. The vibrations of hurry and excitement are foreign to Her atmosphere. And each thing is done not only perfectly, but — as I noticed gradually — in less time than is needed by one in a rush! I have since tried to change my ways and have found that not only is work done better and completed quicker with a mind and temper that is quiet and collected, but the worker himself is not exhausted in the work. The art is to keep the mind free from tension. If that is somehow done then the system does not suffer, life is better lived.

I was strongly reminded of this experience and experiment of mine as I was reading the other day a book[1] by Rear Admiral Shattock in which he describes his search for a system or technique that could give release from the constant tension-producing currents of modern civilisation. He first thought of religion but wisely gave it up as he saw that, among other things, it meant involvement in fresh emotions. He sensed that meditation could be a way out if it was kept free from emotive and religious complications. And it was by 'chance',[2] he says, that he came across a book describing such a course of Meditation conducted at a training Centre in Rangoon, for monks and laymen, by Mahasi Sayadaw. The course looked a simple method of mind-training and was called Satipatthana. The admiral wrote to the authorities asking whether he could be allowed to attend the course and, on receiving a more than encouraging reply, he took leave for 4 weeks from service and joined the Centre.

Mr. Shattock describes with engaging humour how he was first enjoined to undertake to abide by the five preliminary rules, viz.: abstention from killing, stealing, lying, intoxicants, sex. He was advised to avoid unnecessary talk, reduce sleep to four hours a night and give up all reading and writing for the duration. That done, two basic exercises were prescribed. The first was to walk up and down a stretch of about fifty paces. While walking, the attention had to be kept on the movement of each foot as it was lifted, swung forward

---

[1] *An Experiment in Mindfulness* by Rear Admiral E. G. Shattock. Pub. E. P. Dutton & Co., New York.
[2] Of course we know there is no such thing as chance in these matters. What is called 'chance' is simply a cover for a high point reached by the forces behind the surface working out the destiny of man. The so-called chance happenings are really the result of the configuration of karmic and other agencies forging the growth of the soul.

and put down and each of these several movements had to be accompanied by mentally saying 'up', 'forward', 'down' or words to that effect. At the end of the stretch, attention was to be given to stopping, turning and starting again. Thus each act, every movement in the walk had to be separated from the other and concentrated upon slowly, deliberately.

The second exercise was to sit in a relaxed position with the attention riveted on the rising and falling of the abdomen as the breath was inhaled and exhaled. Both these exercises were to be done alternately throughout the day, with intervals of rest, as many times as possible. Though they appeared simple when prescribed, things were found to be pretty difficult at the first touch of practice. The mind would not stay in attention. Thoughts would distract, attention would stray elsewhere. Each time this happened, the novice was advised to make a mental note of the distraction and bring back the mind gently but firmly to the subject of attention. If the distraction persisted, the mind was to be fully turned on the object of distraction till its force was expended.

The meditator was soon to discover that distractions came not only in the form of words, i.e. thoughts, but in the form of pictures, scenes, etc. Next to follow were mysterious itchings, aches and pains in the body. This last phenomenon was explained by Sayadaw, the teacher, in the following way. The body is never at rest. There are always movements, irritations, pricks, brushes, etc., in the physical organism. But normally the mind is so much occupied with the incessant flow of thoughts that unless the disturbances are strong enough they are not singly taken notice of by the mind. In a practice like the Satipatthana, the continuity of thought-process is broken and each small disturbance in the body comes to be noticed by the conscious mind.

Another difficulty, experienced in the sitting exercises, was that the practitioner found himself gradually leaning forward and more forward till he would lose balance and topple.

Sayadaw took it very casually and explained that it was a sign of approaching 'samadhi' and it would pass.

Thus all the exercises that were to be done were aimed at control of the mind by restricting its field of activity for longer and longer periods. With persistence and daily guidance, the admiral arrived at a definite stage of mind-control before the lapse of his four-week period. The thought-activity slowed down gradually. He became conscious of every minute reaction in his mind to the objects outside. His sensitivity was heightened and each sound, sight, touch brought a unique value. There awoke in him a new joy of perception of much that he had missed hitherto. A new rhythm of life began to form itself yielding a continuous refreshment to the body and mind. He became conscious of an immense power in himself following the stoppage of all wasteful effort. The range of his awareness widened enormously and the mind could be turned like a torch on anything he liked. He felt satisfied with the results obtained and wished he could have stayed for a few more weeks to complete the course. The mind got into a constant state of relaxation, the system detensioned.

No doubt Mr. Shattock is aware that this method of meditation — we would call it concentration — is not the only way of acquiring control over the mind and arriving at freedom from tension. We know, for instance, that this object and much more can be achieved by sustained Pranayama. Sri Aurobindo has spoken of the spectacular results that followed his Pranayama sessions in his early days at Baroda. Vivekananda has pointedly stressed the wonderful effect of Pranayama on the mind and the life-energy. The least that one gains from Pranayama is a steady quieting of the mind, a widening and heightening of its range of consciousness and a certain detachment of the being from surface activity. The sadhana of Mantra-Japa is also efficacious in the same direction, particularly in the stamp of Peace that it imparts to the practicant. In our yoga one proceeds by collecting the mind and letting it lie open to the Higher Consciousness which begins to flow into it as a result of the working of the Yoga Shakti to which one surrenders oneself. This Consciousness brings with it its own Quiet, Silence, Peace and, as they settle, the very texture of the mind undergoes a change. That way things are less strenuous and more natural.

Astrology

A kind friend has sent me a book on Occultism. Douglas Hunt, the author of this recent work,[1] has read much, travelled a good deal — both by body and mind — and obviously has had wide experience of men and things. Having been a teacher for nearly three decades, he knows how to make his subject interesting. His approach and his presentation of the several aspects of the theme are those of an open mind aware of both the strong points and the weak of the logical intellect and the physical reason. He arrives at no conclusions but leaves each reader to come to his own on the basis of the data he has assembled in these pages. The variety of topics covered in the discussion is as large as it is interesting. I was particularly attracted by what he has to say on astrology.

One may ask, indeed, what astrology has got to do with occultism. It is a regular science proceeding on verifiable data; it is based on astronomy and mathematics and is laid out with scientific precision. Like most sciences, it deals with the how of things though not with the why. All the same, there are certain features of astrology that do not lend themselves to systematisation e.g., the extent to which the planets affect human affairs, the actual method of their action, and lastly — though not strictly within its field — the means adopted in the ancient traditions to modify, if not to change, the workings of the planets; they are occult, 'hidden' to the physical eye.

In the first place, is there any proof that astronomical factors have any influence on terrestrial phenomena? Mr. Hunt makes a reference to Prof. Piccardi, Director of the Institute of Physics and Chemistry at Florence, who con-

[1] *Exploring the Occult*. (Pan Book)

ducted experiments to ascertain "chemical reactions under exactly similar conditions of time, heat, outside temperature, etc. and has discovered to his surprise that these reactions varied according to the date and place at which they were made. From this he deduced not only that they were influenced by the relative positions of the earth and the celestial bodies, but that the position of the earth must have an influence on our health, our temperament, our thoughts, and our actions, not only individually but collectively."

The author then goes on to mention the studies of Dr. Rudolf Tomaschek, Professor of Theoretical Physics at the University of Munich, and his analysis of the character of the relation that is perceived to exist between astronomical facts and terrestrial events. "The correlation of astronomical facts with terrestrial events is the domain of astrology, be they of physical, chemical, physiological or psychological nature. The truth of such correlations can be demonstrated by statistical methods: that is, the correlations between the positions and aspects of the planets and angles with terrestrial events. Their factual character is beyond doubt."

Is that relation causal or casual? Men like Dr. Jung hold that the 'stars' do not cause events but are *synchronistic* with them. But synchronicity does not mean coincidence. Explains Dr. Tomaschek: "According to this view, the totality of events is regarded as an interwoven unity which operates and is operated upon as a whole, so that no single event can be regarded as the cause and another as the effect, but each is correlated with the other. In other words, simultaneous events correspond to one another. Accordingly the celestial bodies would have to be regarded as the hands of a single clock which indicate the total cosmic situation in which our Earth, with everything in it, is involved."

Giving his own analysis of the problem, Professor Tomaschek considers three possible explanations which are summed up by the author: "(1) That the celestial bodies actually *operate* upon terrestrial events. (2) That the celestial bodies *precipitate* events which are ripe for manifestation. (3) That the celestial bodies *symbolise* organic cosmic forces which are qualitative functions of time and space. This last theory seems to make the greatest appeal to the professor. 'It presupposes an animated universe, a spiritual coherence of the whole cosmos. . . . This is an attitude which comes very close to the views of modern natural science.' "

To put it in our own words, the universe is one Whole. It is an organism and there is a natural relation and interaction among all its constituent members at all levels. Each planet, for instance, exerts its influence upon others. Let us not forget, by the way, that the planet is in a position to radiate its influence because it embodies certain cosmic forces or energies; it may not be alive in the same way as our planet is, but it does represent a formulation of particular forces which have their own part to play in the cosmos. Our earth, being a member in this family of the solar system, is naturally subject to the influences of the other member planets, even as they are open to the influence of or influences from the earth. And this planetary influence acts not only upon the earth in a general way, but also in an individual way on all the lives on earth, and there too not only physically but also psychically. The influence exercised by any planet is determined, among other things, by the position it occupies at a given moment, *vis a vis* the rest. The position of the planets at this moment has its own effect on all that comes into being at this point in time. As pointed out by Jung, "Whatever is born or done at this moment of time has the qualities of this moment of time."

The author cites the results of an investigation carried on by a doctor which revealed a definite relation between the season of birth and the illness of his patients: "To my astonishment, a clear pattern emerged. All my pet asthmatics and bronchial patients were Sagittarians, born between November 23rd and December 20th. . . . The ones I never saw were

Arians, Taurians or Scorpios. . . . I haven't traded my
stethoscope for horoscopes but I do now insist that new
patients give me their birthdays."

And of course everyone knows that mental patients are
most violent at the full moon, that crises in illnesses reach
their peak point on new-moon days.

The influence of the planetary positions, then, is a fact. Sri
Aurobindo observes that there is undoubtedly a constant
action of the Universal energies upon the individual energies
and the planetary action could well be one or the first nodus
of this active relation. The question is whether it is a
determinant or only a sign of determination? Certainly they
are not the cause of all that happens here on earth. "The stars
incline, they do not compel." The position of the stars
indicates the trend in the working of the cosmic forces at the
time of the birth of the subject, the time when a destiny is
launched into life on earth; this conjunction of the forces gives
a particular direction to the energies that are released at that
moment and the subsequent developments normally tend to
follow this impetus. I say normally, because all is not
determined by this factor. In fact destiny itself is a fluid
proposition which is forming and modifying itself at every
moment as a result of the working of forces in the universe.
There are two factors that go into its making. One, the
impetus of the past energies, *karma* or *daiva*, cumulative effect
of previous outputs of energies; the second, is human effort,
purusakara. Destiny is what emerges as a result of the
confluence of these two. It is possible to offset *daiva* up to a
certain point by will, by effort which can erect a new karma
to dissipate and displace the old. It is only if the particular
karma is irreversible, *utkata karma*, that it has to be gone
through, unless there is a super-human intervention from
Above — to that I shall turn later. To come back to the point
of astrology, its advantage, say its advocates, is that it gives a
foreknowledge of what is likely to happen on the basis of

definite planetary data. So forewarned, it is possible if one takes appropriate steps to avert, or at least obviate the effects that are indicated. Mr. Hunt observes: "If we know exactly to what actions or situations our 'stars' — planets actually — incline us, we are forewarned, and thus forearmed. Man has a considerable degree of free will, and many occultists have noticed that as a man becomes more highly evolved, so his planets affect him less and less. Nevertheless our horoscopes can quite clearly show our strengths and our weaknesses — and to know these is half the battle."

I said that it is possible to change one's destiny. How is that done, it may be asked. Well, the first truth about destiny to which Sri Aurobindo and the Mother have drawn repeated attention is that destiny is not something unitary. It is a graded formation like all fundamental things in creation. There are many layers of destiny, many sources of destiny, in fact many destinies themselves. Man is made up of so many personalities, so many beings we may say, each with its own destiny and field. The body has its destiny, the vital has another, the mental has its own and so on. What results in the interaction of all these destinies in force is the operative Destiny. That which is most dominant gains the upper hand. And what dominates depends upon the level of consciousness that one normally lives in, the particular plane of being from which one usually functions, whether it is the physical, vital or mental etc. This is not merely so in the long-run. Even from moment to moment one can see the truth of this fact. As the Mother emphasises, if I remain at the summit of my consciousness — the highest height I have attained — it is always the best that will happen in all circumstances.

It is possible by shifting one's fulcrum in life from one level of consciousness to another, to bring to bear the workings of a new destiny on the old. This invariably happens when one turns to spiritual life. For then one turns in a new direction, a new dimension is added to the field, a new

Force of the spirit begins to act and the lines of the old destiny lose their sharpness. This is not only regarding one's own destiny, but another's as well. I know of at least one authentic case when a certain death was averted by the Japa of the potent *mrityunjaya mantra* by an adept in the mantric lore. By means of *mantrashakti*, by means of one's own tapasya — intensified soul-power — it is possible to release forces which can interrupt the workings of destiny in another and forge a new destiny for him. The individual relates himself to a higher Will, a Will that transcends the realm of human karma and in proportion to its assumption of the control of his life, the hold of the lower destiny is replaced by the higher working. That is why we see that horoscopes and astrological readings which prove so accurate in cases of some persons fail to be so when they turn to spiritual life.

And then there is another great factor which can set at nought karma of any kind, *prarabdha* or *utkata*. And that is the Grace of the Divine. The Grace, whether it acts directly or through the person of one's Guru, comes from the highest plane, beyond the karmic domain, and it is irresistible. It can completely set aside, cancel the karma and negate all astrological predictions. I cannot forget how a couple of years ago an astrologer-friend had warned me that I was in for a serious illness at about a particular date. 'A death-like experience', he repeated, every time he saw me, though he was kind enough to assure that I would scrape through. I told it to the Mother. She looked and laughed; all my clouds melted away. The date came and went and I did not have even my usual 'flu. Later, the Mother asked me with a smile, significantly, if the date had passed.[1] I could multiply so many instances from my personal knowledge when death was strongly forecast, the crises actually arrived, but the

---

[1] In fairness to my astrologer-friend, I must record that a number of his other predictions, especially on the literary and the financial side, have come remarkably true.

calamities were averted by the merciful intervention of the Mother who had been appealed to. The Mother's Grace is, to my knowledge and experience, the surest dissolvent of our karma, the greatest single determinant of what shall be in the world of today.

Dowsing

Like most people, I had never paid thought to any possible rationale that might underlie the phenomenon called dowsing. I had known that there are what are called water-diviners who go about with a forked twig or a pendulum in their hand to find likely spots where water (or minerals) can be found. When they pass over tracts where there is water, the pendulum begins to swing slowly or violently according to the quantity of water that is lying below. These people are no longer treated as pretentious quacks, but are recognised and even employed by Governments to help find out water-springs in scarcity areas. Though I had no personal experience in the matter, I believed in its possibility and attributed it vaguely to some unusual occult capacity with which a few are gifted. Beyond this I never thought of it till the other day when I came across a most interesting — and intriguing — incident reported by Douglas Hunt in his book already referred to. Here it is.

M. Henri Meier of Luxemberg, an eminent radiesthist, was interned by the Nazis during the war and when the camp well dried up, he successfully found a fresh water supply. Now let Mr. Hunt speak.

"A few days later the camp commandant sent for him and ordered him to locate a spring beneath the floor of his office. He would listen to none of M. Meier's protestations that he had already been over the ground and knew there was no water there.

'There is water there and you will find it,' barked the commandant. 'You will start your operations over my desk.'

Reluctantly the unfortunate man got out his pendulum and chart and sat down at the desk. To his amazement the pendulum immediately started rotating, and before long he had worked out that three metres beneath the commandant's desk there was a spring with a capacity of ten litres a minute. He was even more amazed when the commandant burst into a roar of laughter.

'Ah, Herr Meier,' he said, 'that was a little trick I played on you. Look!' and he lifted the blotter on his desk and showed a drawing of a spring. Beneath it were the words: Depth, three metres; capacity, ten litres."

Frankly I was intrigued. What could be the explanation, I asked myself. What was the principle involved in this phenomenon? If only the diagram and the figures had that impact on Meier, could it be the principle of the *yantra* that operated? Otherwise how could the diviner be misled? And Mr. Meier was no novice; he was a renowned authority on his subject. I speculated but I was not satisfied with the many explanations that occurred to my mind and so I approached the Mother with the problem.

What She said is revealing. She said in effect: Usually when these persons set about divining, it is their sub-conscient that informs them. It is not the instrument that is the cause of the discovery. The sub-conscient grasps the knowledge of the existence of the water or mineral and communicates it to the instrument in the hands of the person. This is the first principle. In this particular case the commandant must have made a strong mental formation based upon the drawing and used his vital power to impose that formation on our friend. That is to say, he put a strong spell akin to hypnosis upon the diviner who received that formation in his sub-conscient; the rest followed as a matter of course.

The Mother smiled and remarked that the officer must have been quite a capable man to have done this. And indeed he was. Mr. Hunt's account makes mention of this fact — that the commandant had studied the subject well enough to play tricks of this sort — though I had not spoken of this to the Mother!

Thus it is the person and not the instrument that is the primary factor. As the author puts it well, the instruments "are simply antennae which register the dowser's response to the radiation." All the same, in keeping with the characteristic spirit of modern science and its reliance on physical bases and means, various instruments have been devised so as to function more sensitively and precisely and they have been put to use, particularly in the West, for making diagnosis of illnesses as also for indicating and even radiating the treatment — whether the patient is present or not.[1] With the development of the science of radiesthesia or radionics in the medical circles, laboratories are working upon these instruments with considerable success.[2]

It was during the last War that we had an interesting visitor to the Ashram with a number of novel instruments. He was an officer in the Air Force of a foreign country and had remarkable powers of dowsing. It appears that with the aid of those instruments he would pore over maps and indicate precisely where a pilot had crashed or baled out. Along with the instruments, he used to hold in his hand a piece of

---

[1]But it is essential that something of the patient be there with the radiesthist. "Diagnosis can be made in the absence of the patient with a sample of the patient's blood, urine, or saliva. If this is held in one hand and the pendulum is held over a design of the human body, the pendulum will show by appropriate movement which part of the body is affected."

[2]Best known of these is probably the Delawarr diagnostic instrument, which was developed in the Delawarr Laboratories at Oxford. There is also an instrument for radiating treatment to the patient. Dr. Albert Abrams in the last century was the first to use an instrument of this description. It was developed by Dr. Ruth Brown in the States and by the Delawarr Laboratories in England. The exact basis on which these instruments work is not very clear, but they do enable a diagnosis to be made. It is also said to be possible to find the appropriate remedies. A somewhat similar treatment is supposed to be able to broadcast ultrasonic treatment to the patient in his absence provided a 'sample' — blood , urine, saliva — is connected with the instrument."

Speaking of a personal experience, Mr. Hunt adds: "At one time my own son had 'absent' radionic treatment. Every now and then the radiesthist would ring us up in the morning and say: 'Nigel had a rotten night last night: how did he get that ear-ache?' or something similar. When we asked him how on earth he knew that Nigel had been awake with ear-ache, he would laugh and say: 'I've got a drop of his blood here.'

It sounds, as the man himself remarked, perfectly medieval, but as Mephistopheles said to Faust in Goethe's great occult drama: 'Blut ist ein ganz besonderer Saft.' (Blood is a very special kind of juice.)"

clothing of the person concerned. The authorities would follow his clue and they did find the bodies of the pilots at the places indicated by him. But he was not fully satisfied with the results. He had found in his experience that the instruments did not always guide him aright. He wanted to know the whole rationale behind this phenomenon — in which he was participating without knowing the real how of it — and also why the showings of the instruments went wrong on occasions. Sri Aurobindo was approached on his behalf and shown the instruments etc. Sri Aurobindo pointed out that in these matters the instruments are only secondary; they indicate that the person handling them has a certain capacity to be open to the plane whence proceeds this knowledge. The right and the most effective course for such a person — once he becomes aware of his natural capacity — would be to develop that power by some means — yogic or other — and establish a living and direct contact in his consciousness with that plane so as to be able to receive its knowledge immediately and spontaneously, doing away with dependence upon external means which are liable to be influenced by so many factors, known and unknown.

Tao as a way of Immortality

I think it was in the *Hindu* Magazine Section. They had published, some years ago, a brilliant story of a strange case of hypnotism. It was not clear how far it was based on facts. All the same it produced an indelible impression on my mind and marked a turn in my thinking on the occult side of things. An experienced hypnotist is working on a friend. After the subject is put into a trance, he is asked to narrate the events in his life five years ago; the answers are clear and vivid. Ten years ago; the replies are equally fluent. Twenty years ago, thirty years ago, when he was only five: at this stage the subject starts behaving like an infant of that age and with appropriate gestures speaks falteringly. A hundred years ago; without difficulty the subject tells of happenings in his past birth. Excited by curiosity, the hypnotist asks him what happened two hundred years earlier and then still earlier, till the subject starts jabbering in a peculiar manner and behaving like a monkey. Just at that moment there is a loud explosion in the laboratory and the 'monkey' starts up and jumps out through the window. The hypnotist is alarmed and rushes out pursuing the 'monkey' which cannot be found. The subject under spell goes flying from house-top to house-top, refuses to come back and makes himself scarce. And it is only after a long period of suspense and effort that the 'monkey' is coaxed to come again into the room where he is forcibly put to sleep enabling the hypnotist to work upon him in the reverse direction till the relevant human stage is reached and, to the relief of all, he wakes up as if from deep sleep.

As a sketch of the theoretical possibilities of the technique of hypnotism, the story seemed indeed original, and its purport could not be missed. But I never thought seriously of the practical implications of the matter till the other day when a book, *Le Dominicain Blanc* by Gustav Meyrink, came into my hands.

Gustav Meyrink (1868 - 1932) was an Austrian writer who was considered to be the most notable literary medium in Europe in the last century. Introducing his work, M. Gerard Heym states in his illuminating preface that Meyrink was passionately interested in occult phenomena and his entire life was one long quest for the Esoteric Knowledge of different traditions. He assimilated the knowledge of a special line of Yoga and developed the potentialities of his being to a remarkable extent, acquiring in the process immense powers of clairvoyance and developing capacities to function as a medium to a surpassing degree. He helped many by the exercise of his powers of telepathy, materialisation, etc. But his one preoccupation was always his quest for the Higher Knowledge, the Wisdom of God. He utilised his occult capacities to enter into the original stream of those old traditions which still live in their own formulations some-where in the earth-atmosphere, integrate himself into their flow and even obtain an initiation "as if by reflection in a mirror". That is to say, he projected himself in his subtle body into the influence of the Masters of the chosen tradition — on their own planes of functioning — and sought their instruc-tion. And, we are told, some of the living adepts came to admire him as a 'brother'. It was thus that he acquired a profound degree of knowledge of the ancient traditions, occult and spiritual. But he could not, the writer notes, reach the supreme realisation because his whole life was vitiated by a certain disequilibrium resulting from an excessive hatred for his mother.

The circumstances in which he came to write this book in question are again interesting.

It was in 1870 that three articles on Taoism by Dr. A.

Pfitzmaier, a noted Sinologist, were published in the Austri-an press.[1] The writings caused a great stir and the learned professor was prevailed upon not to pursue the subject further as the general mind of the public was said to be not yet ripe for such a teaching, and no more was heard of it. But Meyrink had read some of them and he was at once fired with enthusiasm powerful enough to lead him to 'contact' the ancient tradition of the Tao.

What is there in Tao, it may be asked, to raise so much furore? What again is the element that is not found in its books but is in the preserve of adepts requiring occult means for communication? M. Heym explains that Taoism, in the first place, is not confined to China. In fact, it is older than the Chinese civilisation. It was in the closing years of the Sung dynasty, when the country was faced with the invasions of the Mongols, that many of the Masters of Tao left the country with their sacred lore to safeguard their heritage and migrated and settled down in more hospitable environments. Similar migrations took place when Confucianism came into ascendency and persecuted the older faith. Some spread themselves in Europe, some in the countries of Islam; it was here in the Islamic regions that the adepts developed and perfected the science of Alchemy which was an integral part of their tradition.

To the layman Tao is a way of deliverance; to the initiate it is a way of Immortality. Like all the ancient traditions, Tao has an esoteric aspect side by side with the exoteric. The esoteric teaching has for its goal the attainment of Immortality and it is meant only for the elite who are considered fit to enter into their order of hierachy.

Now the summit of this pyramid of the esoteric hier-archy consists of adepts called the Immortals, numbering

---

[1]The Real Men and the Immortals in Taoism", "Dissolution of the Corpse and the Sword", "Some Points in Taoism".

about a dozen. Immortality in this context means the immortality of the body by the creation of a subtle body which is almost physical but extremely purified. And this body and the mind that inhabits it stay immortal.

There are several ways for achieving this immortality of the body. One is to use what is known as the elixir of long life, consisting of a mysterious substance with intensely active properties. Another method is a complicated technique of breathing exercises combined with visual concentration upon some of the active centres in the body. Another discipline that has been woven into this process is the tantric technique of a unique union of the two principles in creation, viz. the masculine and the feminine, which precipitated a state of transcendent bliss.

Gustav Meyrink was drawn to esoteric Tao like iron to a magnet and took to his quest with all his customary zeal. He drew upon his clairvoyant powers to seek out the old Masters and put himself into contact with them — Masters in their subtler worlds. He practised and succeeded in identifying himself with the Path to such an extent that he was able to penetrate into its secrets and integrate himself with its current. *Le Dominicain Blanc* is a graphic record of his experiences and realisations in this field in the form of a story.

The way that is sketched out in the narration is known as the Path of Shi-Kiai. It consists of the dissolution of the body, followed by the dissolution of the mystic Sword which makes its appearance on the disappearance of the body, and then the projection of the subtle body which is called the body of resurrection. This new body may become visible or may remain invisible to the gross eye.

M. Heym draws attention to the existence in Europe of the tradition of the dissolution of the body and its reconstitution or resurrection by means of an alchemic process. He cites the instance of the great adept in Germany, Hon. Schmidt (18th century A.D.), who made a successful experiment in this direction. Schmidt had an elixir placed in his coffin. When the physical body was dead his subtle body and mind got disengaged from it and the elixir dissolved the physical body. Thereafter there was the act of palingenesis effected through an alchemic method, utilising the cosmic forces in creation directed by the will of a master-alchemist who, though not on the earth, could still exercise and effectuate his will from his plane because he had attained the status and consciousness of an Immortal. This master created, around the 'envelope' abandoned by the physical body, a body extremely sensitive, with exactly the same form and the same functions as those of the original normal body.

But the Taoists of the tradition here described do not resort to alchemic means for the dissolution of the body. They do this by means of their own processes of control and direction of life-breath. The dissolution proceeds through a series of steps culminating in a state of 'nothingness'. Then commences the process of re-creation by the exercise of the will and the special technique perfected by them. This progressive transformation of the living body into an immortal body could be effected equally, as stated earlier, by the profound Tantric process based on the union of the male and the female principles in creation. This technique of the Tantra is linked by the Taoists to their own method of breathing exercises. And it is this combination which is described in its operation by Meyrink in his interesting story built round the figure of Colombier who arrives at his goal of immortality with the aid of Ophelia, his 'sister-soul', who dies with a purpose, gets assimilated in her femininity with the masculine in the hero and helps him to emerge into a new state of perfection.

Life behind Life

A near relation had appeared for a competitive examination. He was a brilliant student and had been called for the *viva voce*. But he had a severe handicap of stammer and so, while conveying his prayers for Blessings to the Mother, I had drawn Her attention to this disability of his. The *viva voce* was smoothly got through. He wrote to say that not once had he stammered throughout the interview — an amazing phenomenon. But what followed is very interesting. For two hours afterwards he stammered uncontrollably, in a way he had never known before.

This recalled to us the many occasions when the Mother's stopping of rain for a period of time was followed by an unusually heavy downpour immediately afterwards. Is it possible to stop rain? it will be asked. Most certainly yes. It is not only a possibility, but an actuality, as we have seen it here several times. So many times, whether on the eve of an important collective function or of a work like harvesting in the fields, when it threatened to rain and the Mother was appealed to, the rain was stopped till things were completed. No doubt, like the stammer, the suspended forces rushed with double impetus once the check was removed, but that was only to be expected.

The truth is that phenomena like rain, wind, tide, are governed by certain elements or beings at the head of the forces that actuate the phenomena. If one knows how to contact them, influence them, exercise power over them, it is possible to regulate the activities in question. These elements or beings are not always as fierce and demoniac as made out in some of the legends. They have an interesting side too, even a human one. There are among them some who are impish and delight in small inconveniences but are generally amenable to persuasion. Many will remember how once on the Sports Ground of the Ashram when the athletics were in progress and the Mother was present noting down the results — as She used to do during those days — it darkened in the skies and threatened to rain. The Mother spoke to the beings concerned that they had better not rain. When they demurred, She told them that in any case She would not use the umbrella but would continue to sit in the open even if it poured. It drizzled a little, the Mother did not move nor did She allow the use of the umbrella. The drizzling stopped and the skies cleared.

But there are rules of the game. We have seen the Mother at times sitting in the open watching the children's functions when it was pouring in torrents. Why did She not stop the rains? Could She not compel the elements to stop? It is not always a question of what is possible or not possible but of what is advisable or not advisable in a given set of circumstances. On the particular occasion I am speaking of, as I learnt later, the Mother deliberately did not intervene. There are occasions when it is best to let things work out in their own way; any interruption or contradiction simply worsens matters. It was the time when all kinds of huge explosions — atom bombs, hydrogen bombs and other nuclear blasts — were being carried out with gusto. As a result of them, it appears, the hitherto established and existing harmony in the organisation of Nature had been severely disturbed and the various elements, beings and other subtle physical participants in the cosmos had been thrown into a vortex of confusion. They were like mad and rushing about doing what they liked. The floods, quakes and other disasters that were happening at that time were largely due to this factor. They were thus best left to themselves as otherwise their pent-up fury would have precipitated yet greater havoc once the holds were removed.

Our ancients had a deep knowledge of the organisation of the universe. All creation was to them of one piece. There is one Truth, one Principle that is severally formulated. Whether it is in the individual or in the universal, the Truth that finds expression is the same. The organisation of both follows the same lines. In fact there is a close interrelation of correspondence between the two. That is why it is possible for the individual, by a particular system of stresses in his consciousness, to produce certain results in the universal consciousness. Patanjali describes the different kinds of concentration of consciousness, *samyama*, which yield knowledge of corresponding fields of activity in Physical Nature and promote a simultaneous power of control over them. The Tantras have developed a system in which it is possible by yoga to become conscious in oneself of the fundamental principles, *tattwas*, in creation and, by a prescribed process, possible too to *dissolve* each *tattwa*[1], i.e. to emerge out of the hold of that *tattwa*, and so acquire a control over it which can be exercised in that poise of consciousness both within the body and outside.

The mystics of the Veda had an intimate experience of this relation as also of the truth of higher beings and cosmic Force-heads presiding over all phenomena in Nature — outer as well as inner. They called them Deities, *devatas*, and gave them Names like Indra, Agni, Maruts, etc. They had their own words of Call, hymns of appeal to the Deities who were in control of their respective spheres of activity both in the objective and the subjective universe. With the aid of these Words of Power they succeeded in getting the Gods to participate in the life-journey of the humans. These hymns of spiritual origin are potent even today in spite of the long lapse of time since they were first formulated in human language. I may cite an instance or two within my personal knowledge.

---

[1]Earth, Fire, Water, etc.

Sri Vasishtha Ganapati Muni, the well-known Poet-Yogin who had achieved a unique synthesis of the Veda and the Tantra in his inner life, was camping in a village in the country-side near our place. The annual harvesting had been just over and all over the village grounds were lying scores of haystacks. He was there in a small house with a few of his devotees. One day, suddenly, someone noticed that a big fire had started in one of the stacks and, fanned by a strong wind, it was rapidly spreading. In great consternation he cried out: "Sire, sire, save us. Borne by the wind this fire will soon burn us all to ashes. There is no way of escape; save, save!" The sage heard the call of distress with composure, grasped the situation and proceeded to invoke the Grace of God Agni. In his thrilling voice, he chanted aloud the Rik of Parashara:

Vanema purviraryo manisa agnih,
susoko visvanyasyah.

(May we win the many Riches, may the Fire, flaming high with his light, master by the thinking mind, take possession of all things that are.)[1]

Instantaneously, both the fire and the wind turned in another direction and all was saved. That very night the Muni composed a fresh hymn to Agni, to express his gratitude to the Deity.

I recall yet another incident in which the same personage is concerned. It was during this same period that his son, who had come from the South to meet him, was involved in a motor accident and got a fracture of the arm. Medical facilities were not immediately available in that dense forest where the party had camped. The Muni thereupon had recourse to a Vedic mantra which is celebrated as an *astra*, an unfailing super-natural weapon, for the healing of joints.

---

[1] *Rig Veda*, I, 70, 1.

The Mantra summoned was a Rik of Kanva Medatithi addressed to Indra:

> *Ya rte cidabhisrisah pura jatrubhya*
> *atrdah sandhata sandhim maghava*
> *puruvasuriskarta vihrutam punah.*

(He without even ligature, before the spurt of blood from the broken part, closes up the wound, most opulent Maghavan, who maketh whole what is sundered.)[1]

With the force of his own tapasya he enlivened the power stored in the Mantra and delivered the situation into its hands. Very soon the results were patent; the speed and the perfection of the healing that followed amazed every one, the medicos included.[2]

Thus whether by superior power or by persuasion or by appeal to the presiding deities or beings, it is possible to influence the course of events, particularly, natural phenomena. But it is not enough to have the power. One needs to have an adequate spiritual consciousness for its proper use.

---

[1] *Rig Veda*, VIII,1,12.
[2] These and other interesting incidents are recorded in the biography of the sage, *Vasistha Vaibhavam*, by Sri Kapali Sastriar.

Prayer

This is a first-hand report by a practising surgeon which appeared recently in the press. One day an aged muslim lady arrived at a hospital with her ailing grandson in a push cart. The doctor saw the patient and found him beyond recovery. It was a case of a severe illness requiring spinal operation but with practically no chances of recovery at that stage. Still, in response to the pleadings of the old lady, he had the patient taken to the operation theatre. When he was being removed, the lady knelt down in a praying posture. The operation took its usual time and the patient was brought back to the ward and left on a cot. The lady was still kneeling in the same posture. The doctor went home, leaving routine instructions with the nurse in charge to report to him after a few hours. Truth to say, he expected to hear that the patient had died. Imagine his surprise when he received the phone call in the evening to say that not only was the patient living, but there were definite signs of improvement. The doctor got curious and went to the hospital to find the old lady still in prayer. Since morning she had been in that position. He felt the pulse of the patient, confirmed to himself the reading of the assistant and then tapped the old lady. She looked up with a face that caused strange emotions in the doctor. He told her that the boy had come round and was improving. The lady burst into tears and said, "Praise be to Allah!"

Instances of this kind can be multiplied in evidence of the intervention of new or unknown factors leading to recoveries that would be normally impossible. We read in history how, when prince Humayun was seriously ailing, his father, Babar, prayed to God to shorten his own life and extend Humayun's instead; and as events turned out, Humayun recovered and Babar's health gradually failed. We were reminded of this occurrence when some years ago — it is 30 years now — a devotee wrote to the Mother appealing to Her to save his father's life which was in danger and shorten his own correspondingly. The father recovered. But on coming to know of his son's prayer to the Mother which had been offered without his knowledge, he was gravely perturbed and wrote to the Mother imploring Her to restore to his son his full span of life, adding that he was prepared to forfeit his extended lease of life in the process. Sri Aurobindo sent him a gracious reply assuring him that things were not done on such mathematical bases and conveyed to them His Blessings.

So many questions arise. Is it really possible to arrest or change the course of events by the power of prayer? If so, what happens to the law of Karma? Can you interfere with its operations by means of prayer? Or, in other words, is it possible to change the workings of Nature by individual prayer?

There are indeed many sides to this complex question. But there is one central truth to which all else is subsidiary. There is one Will at work in the universe. And that Will is not a mechanical something, but a divine conscient Will. All Karma, all individual wheels of karma form a part of the process of this Will. And this Will moves through a working out of the infinite possibilities which it directs to the destined goal. The Will is not a static factor pre-determined in its operations. It is a dynamic Power which takes into account the innumerable factors and forces which come into being from moment to moment and varies its workings accordingly. It is possible, says Sri Aurobindo, to get into contact with it, to touch it, to invoke it, to exert a pull on it through means like concentration, prayer, aspiration. That is to say, the human will can, through some means or other, attune and even link itself to the greater Will and move it to function according to its own seeking. The response of the higher Will is what we call the Grace. The Higher consents to be moved by the lower.

Thus, prayer is a means to establish a communication with the Divine Will. The more intense and concentrated it is, the quicker it reaches its destination and fulfils its purpose. But this is not to say with the Mimamsakas that by means of prayers or rituals embodying the prayers, man can compel the Vidhi (Fate) to act as one desires. The Higher Will has its own large lines and objective. Whether it responds or does not respond ultimately depends upon whether what is sought for harmonises with its Purpose or does not.

Potency of the Mantra

I had taken a young friend to the Mother. There was somebody else ahead of him offering *pranams* and he stood aside waiting for his turn. As he was thus standing, he repeated within himself a Mantra which he was using for long. The Mantra was addressed to the Supreme Divine Mother and to his surprise, the Mother looked up in his direction as he repeated the Mantra. He was taken aback; for the Mother was fully engaged with the person in the front and She had suddenly lifted Her head and looked up. The surprise and joy of it, however, were temporary. For the next moment, a doubt — the ubiquitous doubt which comes in on all such happy occasions to rob the glory and reduce the gains — raised its head and whispered, 'It may be a coincidence!' But the gentleman was not to be denied. To test matters, he repeated the Mantra; again the Mother looked up. In his confirmed joy he repeated it a third time, and for the third time did the Mother look up with a faint smile.

This incident brought home to me so many aspects of the matter. First, that the Mother does take cognisance of calls addressed to any Divine Form hallowed in the Scripture. Second, the Mantra is a living word of call. Third, it is possible even today in the 20th century to utilise effectively these Mantras of ancient origin dating back to more than a thousand years. Of course we all know that for the Rishis of the Veda the Mantra was a potent means to communicate with the Gods. The Epics are full of narrations of how the heroes in their battles with the adversary resorted to the use of specific Mantras while discharging their arrows, thereby endowing those weapons with uncommon efficacy. The Ramayana describes how Rama was initiated in this science, even in his infancy, by Rishi Vishwamitra communicating the Vidyas of *Bala* and *Atibala.* Even in comparatively recent history there are recorded happenings in the lives of saints and sages testifying to the potency of the Mantra. I have referred elsewhere to a notable incident in the life of Sri Raghavendra Swami (16th century A.D.) but it bears repetition in the present context.

It appears Parimalacharya — as he was known before he assumed the pontificate — was once passing through a town in the course of his tours and happened to rest in a corner of a palatial house of an official where a big ceremony was in progress. The itinerant had just taken his bath and was doing his *parayana,* devotions, away from the crowd that had gathered. At that time he came to the notice of a priest who was looking-out for someone handy to grind enough sandal paste to suffice for the large number of guests that were present.[1] The functionary asked him peremptorily to get the paste ready. The traveller, poor that he was, had but to agree. He started rubbing the sandalwood on the stone with a little water, while continuing his muttered recitation of the Mantras in which he had been engaged. At that moment the Mantras he was repeating happened to be hymns addressed to Agni. The paste got ready, the priest collected it and at the proper time it was passed round among the guests who helped themselves liberally and applied it on their bodies. Immediately there was a commotion. All who had used the paste complained of heat, unbearable heat in the body and screaming ensued. Enquiries were made and the priest was called in. He got flustered and realised what must have happened. He recalled that the man whom he had asked to prepare the paste had been reciting an Agni Sukta and

---

[1]It is a practice in the warmer parts of the South to use this paste on the body to eliminate heat.

understood that he must have been a Mantra Siddha. Apologies followed and entreaties made to the guest to forgive and set things right. Parimalacharya was embarrassed, for he had not intended what had happened. He felt genuinely sorry, excused himself before the assembly, took the rest of the paste from the plate, chanted the Varuna Sukta, hymn addressed to Varuna, the Deity of Water, and passed round the charged paste. Needless to say it gave the needed relief to all.

The Mantra has a power, is a power. But it is not a power everywhere, always and to everyone. There are conditions in which alone the Mantra becomes vibrant with power. In the first place, the Mantra must proceed from a Source of Power. The Inspiration or the Revelation that causes the Mantra to come into being must be of a higher, spiritual order. It is not as if an idea is taken and then words found to clothe the idea in a particular metre. Along with the awakening to a Truth in Idea or in Form, there comes from the depths or from some heights certain sounds or words giving sound-expression to that Truth which is generally called the Deity embodying that particular manifestation of the Truth. This is the real Mantra, instinct with an innate consciousness-force which can manifest the Truth or the Deity from which it derives when it is properly operated upon. So done, the Mantra not only invokes the presence of the Deity in a subtle way, but there are at times unmistakable physical effects of that Presence.[1] When Sri Kapali Sastriar was doing the *upasana*, prescribed adoration, of Sri Matangi, the Divine Mother presiding over the harmonies of Speech, parrots would fly in and settle on his arms. And it did not really surprise him, for Matangi is lauded in the Scripture as holding the parrot in Her hands, *kira-hasta*.

---

[1] It is on record, how when Vasishtha Ganapati Muni was composing, under the drive of an irresistible Inspiration, his famous hymns to Indrani, Goddess of Illumination and Rain (of plenty), the skies used to be overcast with clouds and lightning and showers break out though it was full summer at that time.

But this intrinsic power, *mantra-shakti*, is not all. It is usually latent. It needs a live agency to awaken that power and transmit the mantra in that condition to another. This is done by the Guru who awakens the potency by his own *tapas-shakti*, force of askesis, and imparts it to the disciple, so that it becomes a living Mantra to him. Of course, theoretically it is possible for a seeker to energise the potency of a Mantra by the force of his own tapas and make it a live factor in his being. But that is rare.

After the Mantra is given, it is up to the disciple to keep it alive, nourish it and make it an effective force in his own being by means of his *sādhana-shakti*, power of inner culturing. He has to take steps to make that mantra natural to himself, a part of his own being so that it functions as spontaneously as the living breath.

It is pertinent to consider at this stage the oft-asked question whether it is indispensable to follow the meaning of the Mantra while repeating it. This question is raised because it happens at times that the Mantra does fructify even when the practicant is not conscious of the meaning while repeating it. All Shastras lay it down that the meaning of the Mantra must be understood in full; not only understood, but followed step by step while repeating the sounds or words that formulate it. Patanjali is clear on the point: *tad japah, tad artha bhavanam*, — repetition of the Mantra, and dwelling upon the meaning of the Mantra. What makes up for the lack of this requirement is a strong faith on the part of the practitioner in the Mantra. The inherent power of the Mantra, the Influence of the Guru active in the Mantra and the faith of the sadhaka, all combine to achieve results. But this is not a rule.

Another point. It is not that anyone can take up any mantra. It is facilely assumed that all Mantras being words of call to the Divine, any one of them is as good as any other and one can choose what one likes. But it is not so. I came to realise this truth one day when the Mother made an observation. A devotee had complained that a simple Mantra given to him by a saint and repeated by him with devotion had caused much disturbance in his system. It was a Mantra addressed to Sri Rama. But each time he practised it, there was a peculiar contra movement in the pit of the stomach and he felt uneasy. He was bewildered and wondered how a mantra that gave solace to so many could have this result in him. The moment I spoke of it to the Mother, She replied that it was obvious the Mantra was not a friendly Mantra (to him). This opened a world of meaning to me. The full significance flashed of the instructions in the Tantra treatises regarding the necessity of a careful choice and the manner in which the Mantra is to be selected for the disciple. The Guru is enjoined to observe and study carefully the nature of the prospective disciple; to ascertain his horoscopic background, the indications of his previous development and present possibilities; and on the basis of all these data, to determine which particular Mantra would be suitable to him.

Animals

Nagod in Uttar Pradesh was the scene, some years ago, of a remarkable happening which has been recently featured by a prominent Weekly in Kannada. Here is the report:

He was a prisoner doing a stretch for some offence. Of a frightening visage, he could be counted upon being a bugbear to little children. But he enjoyed a reputation as a *Mantrika*, especially famed for bringing snake-bitten victims back to life. Once a man was bitten by a black viper. Even before he could be removed to the hospital, the victim had turned blue; his limbs had gone cold.

Doctors worked on the patient all night but were unable to draw out the poison from his system. Finally they gave up and pronouncing the man dead, returned the body.

With a slight of hope that the Mantrika might effect a miracle, the body was taken to the jail where the prisoner was lodged. The jail authorities knew the prisoner's unusual power on snakes and their deathly bites and had given him standing permission to go out to treat patients who sought his ministrations.

The Mantrika came out, examined the victim and proceeded to collect a few details of the viper that had dealt the mortal blow. Then he took out a few black-grams from his vest pocket and with an incantation began throwing them on the body. Nothing happened; the body lay cold, lifeless.

He would not give up. He commissioned a dish of milk and even before it arrived, drew three large concentric circles. The body was placed in the innermost circle, the dish of milk in the second and the by-standers were asked to stay in the outer circle, with an injunction not to move out of the circle or to panic.

Incanting, he went round the circle once and thereafter continued to repeat the mantra. After a while he took out two coins from his pocket and uttering a magical formula threw them up. Where they landed, none knew, none saw.

Half an hour passed; the Mantrika was all a tremble with rage. Nonetheless the incantation continued without pause or respite. Then the bystanders saw, in abject terror, a black viper approach the outer circle and with its angry open hood begin to rap the ground. The two coins the Mantrika had thrown up were stuck to the adder's hood.

"Are you in distress?" enquired the Mantrika. And, as if in confirmation, the snake nodded its hood. In a futile struggle to dislodge the coins it was repeatedly striking its hood on the floor.

"If you want them gone, you had better set about drawing the poison away from the man's body" — these were the terms of the Mantrika to the reptile.

But it would not listen. It continued its antics with the hood. Now the Mantrika was indeed roused. He demanded a yard of new cloth and when it was brought to him, he made it into the shape of a snake, but not before he had offered yet one more chance to the adder to relent. It did not yield. The Mantrika then tore a bit of the cloth — which now resembled a snake — at the tail, incanting his formula at the same time. And strange! Blood gushed forth from the tail of the live snake, sending a wave of terror into the hearts of the crowd. The viper's obstinacy enraged the Mantrika still further. He now tore another inch from the tail of his cloth-snake and the live snake's tail too was seen cut and bleeding. The snake had perforce to admit defeat. Slowly it approached the body and going round once, and then again for the second time, it sought the place where the man had been bitten and began to suck the poison out. In about half an hour's time, the colour of the body began to change; in a short while the man started breathing and soon got up as if from a deep sleep.

Allowing for certain possible embellishments inevitable in reportings of this type, there is nothing at all improbable in this account. For it is a fact that one can acquire power over the animal world by means of the Mantra. Each class of animals, e.g. snakes, dogs, scorpions etc., has its own group-life and its own group-being. We may call it the spirit or the deity of that species. It is possible to propitiate this spirit by occult means such as rites that are prescribed in the occult lore of all lands, and through it obtain control over the particular creation. It is also possible to gain this contact by means of *mantra-upasana*. There are special Mantras which, when successfully practised and realised, endow the practitioner with power to control the forces of beings that preside over their respective domains. One may gain some contact, enter into a relation and seek the favour of that spirit. Or one may acquire a power of control over it and through it, over the creation ruled by it. The latter would seem to be the case with our Mantrika. By a combination of Mantra and Kriya (ritual), he exercised a compelling power on the snake-world and — in the incident under report — compelled the snake to withdraw the poison it had injected into the victim.

It may be noted that his preparing a cloth replica of the snake closely corresponds to the recognised technique in black art of this type, of using a likeness or some personal belonging of the person concerned to act upon him. Though it is indeed possible to strike one without any such medium, it is easier to act through concentration on a material object which, by reason of having absorbed the personal vibrations of the intended victim or through likeness of the victim's form, serves as an effective channel.

There is another kind of relationship which one may establish with these animal types; it is one of friendship, of understanding. And, it is amazing to note, that once an understanding is arrived at, they keep to it much more faithfully than their human superiors. Sastriar once related to me an incident in his life; it was about scorpions. Scorpions, as we all know, are frequent visitors in tropical countries and the more hot it is, the more frequent are their visitations. Their sting is excruciatingly painful and at times even fatal. Many of these scorpions used to enter Sastriar's house. He arrived at an understanding with them that he would not harm them and they on their part left him alone. Times without number he would be suddenly startled out of his preoccupations — whether sitting or walking — to see a scorpion leisurely sauntering about or sitting watching him. But they never touched him. Things went on this way for a long time. One day, however, some relations arrived in the house with plenty of children. And when a scorpion was seen moving about during this period, Sastriar's mother told him that it would be better to kill it as there were so many children exposed and the risk was not worth taking. Sastriar demurred. But she persisted and spoke to him again and again. Reluctantly he yielded and the scorpion was destroyed. And imagine, the next day another scorpion came into Sastriar's room and for the first time he was stung!

Not only have animals a code of honour of their own, but they also have a remarkable faculty of entering into the spirit and mind of their human companions. A colleague of mine from abroad was describing the other day how he had a darling of a dog which sensed his moods even before he expressed them. If he happened to be depressed for any reason, it would lie on the carpet at a distance from his seat and go on gazing at him with a half-turned look. If he happened to be cheerful, it would jump on his sofa, caress him with its paws and add a joyous note to the atmosphere.

Some of the animals are sensitive spiritually too. Cats, for instance, are very receptive to spiritual vibrations. They are found to be very susceptible to spells of meditation. It was obviously one such cat that moved Sri Aurobindo into this portrayal:

Mute stands she, lonely on the topmost stair,
An image of magnificent despair;
The grandeur of a sorrowful surmise
Wakes in the largeness of her glorious eyes.
In her beauty's dumb significant pose I find
The tragedy of her mysterious mind.
Yet is she stately, grandiose, full of grace.
A musing mask is her immobile face . . .
An animal creature wonderfully human,
A charm and miracle of fur-footed Brahman.

Early Morning Hour (I)

The early-morning hour, *brahmi-muhurta*, they say, is the best time for meditation. Masters in the spiritual path advise getting up still earlier from bed because it is during these early hours that the uprush of subconscient movements is the greatest and an aspirant would do well to remain awake at this period. Besides, all environmental Nature is at rest and everything is conducive to silent meditation.

I have been following this wise principle for years. Now, after meditation there is a strong tendency to go to sleep for however short a time. I have been advised to resist this pull as it provides a splendid opportunity for the forces of the nether world to rush up and swallow as much as possible the gains made in the consciousness during meditation. I have not yet been able to act up to this always, though each time I have slept thus, there have been chaotic dream-movements and a dull ache in the body. This morning I was shown vividly the truth of the advice.

I stretched myself after meditation, 'for a few minutes'. Naturally I passed into sleep. There in a room I found myself with two visitors who had come uninvited and were busy helping themselves to food. Both were short in stature, reddish in hue, unclothed. They looked like boys but their heads were big, old and lined with age. A most unpleasant sight! I asked them to go. They would not move but went on eating. I told them loudly to depart, they would not budge. Then it occurred to me that they were hostiles and only Mother's Name would have effect. So I called out and repeated Her Name. They got up. I went on repeating Mother's and Sri Aurobindo's Names; they moved out slowly and, with Their Names on my lips, I followed them to the door and saw them leave.

Who were they? I presume unwelcome guests from the subconscient who had come to rob and feast on the bounty received earlier during Meditation.

Early Morning Hour (II)

The hardest of lessons are forgotten. Primitive nature has a thousand ways of wiping out gains of experience and asserting its own ways again and again.

So in spite of the last dream, I relapsed after some time once again into the habit of sleeping 'just for a few moments' after meditation. And sure enough I was once again shown what I was doing.

I found myself in a new place across the railway lines. It was all foreign and I wanted to rush back to the Ashram immediately. It was a long way and I looked for a rickshaw. Rickshaws were there in plenty — a whole row of them — but there was none to pull them. I looked round and saw them in a peculiar way. There was a parapet wall against which the rickshaw pullers were kneeling with their foreheads touching the wall. They were snoring, fast asleep. They were all hefty and exuded a heavy feeling of inertia. It was oppressive. I woke up to realise what a tamasic region of subconscience I had sunk into.

Weeks after this experience, old Adam once again reared his head this morning. I stretched myself. Suddenly I found (in dream) that all the doors of the house were open. Locks had been opened and within a few minutes our valuables stolen. Thieves had broken in and robbed me of my gains.

Chink in the Armour

It is a matter of common experience that we are braver in dreams than in life. We do things there which are beyond us in our waking state. We fly, we fight, we perform somersaults which amaze us on recollection. All that is possible because in dreams it is our vital being that is active: we function largely in the vital body whose resources and power are far greater than those of our physical body. But dreams also reveal chinks in our armour. Things which lie concealed in our waking consciousness come up to the surface and are exposed in all their nakedness.

Once in a dream I saw a huge tiger coming in my direction. I had nothing in my hands to defend myself with and even if I had anything I doubt if I could have made use of it, for I am a born physical coward. Spontaneously I remembered the Mother and called Her. The beast drew back. Again it advanced; again I called the Mother and it went back. A third time, a fourth time, it came, I called, and the tiger withdrew. For the fifth time it started coming. Surprisingly a doubt arose in my mind: 'Supposing my call does not work this time!' That very moment the tiger came upon me and struck on my arm.

The next day when I narrated this to the Mother, She heard me intently and asked: 'Any marks left on the arm? At times they leave a mark.' Luckily no physical marks were left. Only my state of faith was exposed as vulnerable, to enable me to perfect it.

SECTION TWO

LETTERS ON YOGA-SADHANA

The Choice and
Course of Sadhana

It really depends upon what you want to make of your life. Now you have arrived at a stage when you can take stock of yourself, look back and see in what direction your natural faculties have been pointing, discover what were just enthusiasms of the moment and what have been the imprints of your true mission in life. You are also in a position to make a dispassionate appraisal of the strong points and the weak in your make-up, how far the body is capable of supporting the mind and the vital being, to what extent your mind and will are developed and how far they are ready to co-operate with the heart. You have a measure of your nature, a glimpse if not a sufficient look into the soul in your best moments. It is time that you decide what you want to be in this life. And whatever you want, be assured, it is possible to achieve it here in the Mother's environs.

I wonder if I ever told you of a sage observation made by an unlettered lady who was here for a number of years. It is amazing how the unsophisticated get at the heart of things with a facility that is denied to the sophisticated. One day a person from her own village happened to come to the Ashram; he had his own ideas of what ashrams are or should be and naturally he was bewildered by what he saw here. So he went to this lady who had been here sufficiently long and asked her opinion and help to understand things in the Ashram. The lady smiled and told him: "Look here, the Mother is a Kalpa Vriksha (wish-yielding tree). Each one here can get what he wants. If you want peace of mind, you get it; if you want to improve your health, there are more facilities here than anywhere else and there is Her spiritual help also; if you want to learn, you can learn to any lengths; if you want to lead an easy life, enjoy yourself in the material way, you can do that also; if you want God you can get Him too; the Mother's Yoga-shakti is vibrating all over and yoga becomes easy."

And it is so. The Mother has given full freedom to everyone to shape his own life and Her help and support are there ever extended. She has here organised a Centre of life where one is assured of the minimum wants and enough liberty is there for each individual to do what he will with the opportunity that is given him by Providence. Life in freedom, progress in freedom, change by choice: these are features in the Ashram that none can miss.

With this background it is for you to come to a firm decision as to what you will do in the best and the more mature span of your life that is now opening. If you feel it is enough to live in quiet happiness, it is easy to do so. Thanks to the Mother's Grace all things are conducive to this. You do not have to come into contact with elements not congenial to your nature; you can choose such company and such things as are pleasing to you, participate in activities that make you happy. Reasonable care of your physical health, avoidance of strain of any kind and an easy occupation in things that interest you are enough. You can spend the rest of your life in reasonable comfort and peace. If only your soul will allow it!

I say this because certain souls have not taken birth to live a contented creature life, particularly those that have come here to the Mother. Most of these have been waiting for this hour to take birth. For this is a unique period in the history of Man and represents a confluence of forces and movements that have been gathering for ages; this is a moment of the highest spiritual and deepest occult significance and I have been repeatedly assured that such an opportunity will not come again for a thousand years. Beings have flocked here and are continuing to do so. So many people come here, but they really do not know what brings them and why. But He who draws them knows. Unknown to them their souls receive the touch that sets them on the high road to liberation and transformation. Some day, some life, they will arrive, sooner than otherwise.

This being so, it would be natural to expect a person of your type — refined in the sattvic grain — to take to the Yoga of Sri Aurobindo which forms the backbone of the Ashram and provides the Ideal of a divine humanity to the modern world. It is such a big Ideal, you may say, and entertain doubts about your capacity to practise the yoga with any measure of success. True, the ideal of transformation is high, higher than any held up in the past and difficult of achievement. But whoever said that it can be achieved by human effort? It is not the strength or the weakness of a man that is going to determine the results in this endeavour: it is the Supreme Grace at work for the purpose that will effectuate. Be that as it may, the stage of transformation comes only last in this Yoga. There are many antecedent stages, indispensable prior realisations, that are to be worked out before one can think of transformation or the supramentalisation that makes it possible. Let us therefore set to ourselves a comparatively limited and immediate objective: the union with the inner Divine. Mind you, though this is only the first crucial step here in the Yoga of Sri Aurobindo and the Mother, providing the foundation for the subsequent edifice, it is the end of many lines of yogic effort in the old way. It is not easy of achievement but given the necessary effort, the help of the Guru and the Grace of the Divine, it is possible to achieve it in one life-time.

You may choose this practical — may I say immediately practicable? — objective. To become aware of a divine presence within you, to deepen that awareness by psychological and other disciplines into a steady consciousness of the

Divine within, which in turn can lead to union with that inner Divine — this is the broad picture you should have in your mind. And once you decide on it, you should organise your whole life around that purpose. What you think, what you feel, what you do — all must have a relevance, a reference to this inner seeking for the Divine. What helps and promotes this inner search and effort should be welcomed, entertained and utilised; what dampens, blunts or has a contrary effect on the aspiration and its workings should be naturally rejected. As the Mother says, this means the exercise of your will at every moment: for the choice is presented to you at every minute and you are called upon to decide whether you will throw your weight on the side of your aspiration or on the side of desire and ego at every step in your life. There are no small things and big things in Yoga; all are equal occasions to make or mar your future.

To come back to the point. You can choose any door of entry into the kingdom of God. To each, Nature provides a means most fitted for his development and type. To one it may be the faculty in the mind seeking for the delivering knowledge, to another it may be a causeless welling up of devotion to God in the heart. You have to look into yourself and decide which way is natural to you and then take steps to tread that path.

But there are certain preliminaries that are to be observed before the journey proper is begun. For all yoga, says Patanjali, a prior purification is indispensable. He lists eight limbs of self-discipline under the heads of *yama* and *niyama* which every seeker has to practice and perfect before he is fit for further effort. This requirement is not separately proclaimed in this Yoga because it is presumed that those who seek to practise it are perforce equipped in this regard. Also required is a general benevolence in the being creating the right condition for the flowering of the yogic seed. Here too Patanjali enjoins upon the novice friendliness toward the happy, compassion for the unhappy, delight in the virtuous, and indifference to the wicked.

Happily, you do not need to cultivate these qualities. You have them as your natural equipment. What you need is not so much internal purification — you have it already — but an organisation of your consciousness and life. Start at some point, at any point that you feel strong in you and that could be the means of advance. Let it be the main note of your daily life. All other phases should subserve; they should be so organised as to feed your main preoccupation.

Let us take music for instance. It is born with you, it is your second nature and wells up spontaneously in you. When a thing is so dominant it is a sure sign that that is your means of linking with the soul. Approach music in that spirit. It shall no more be an accomplishment to be acquired and perfected, but a golden thread gifted by the Divine to draw you to Him. Make music a sadhana. Leave aside its external frame for the time being; technique and other details are not so important in this setting. Know that the soul of music, *nada*, is the body of Brahman. Take up the *nada*, the sound-vibration, and follow attentively, reverently and lovingly. Mark that the vibrations must be followed up even after the physical notes end; the vibrations in the subtler air are the real link. Wait upon them with all your being. The Sound itself will gradually lead to its Source, to its "point" of origin and disappear, leaving you in the Presence of That of which it was the Sound-Symbol. It is not a few that have touched the depths of the Soul on the line of *nada*. The entire consciousness gets used to focussing itself on the sound and losing itself in the rhythms of the sound; the culmination of this movement is *laya*, absorption. Naturally a discipline like this cannot be practised in the form of a fixed routine for so many hours a day or night. It is a continuing movement which is always at the back of the active consciousness and takes in everything that feeds its harmonies. It goes without saying that music is not an end in itself, but is a means, a joyous discipline that quietens the unrest in nature, soothes the nervous channels and takes you aglide to the Master of Harmonies within.

You can use any opening or openings that present themselves to you. There is, for instance, the aspiration for knowledge which can be easily turned to capital use. You are always athirst for fresh bits of knowledge, in science, in sociology, in so many branches of human understanding. Channelise that aspiration into a seeking for the Knowledge which is the Source of all knowledge. Read the works of those who have realised the Truth, for their works are full of the power of what they have realised. Luckily for us we have the oceanic literature of Sri Aurobindo throwing light upon every conceivable question or problem in human life; there are the unbelievably simple, direct and lucid writings of the Mother touching every aspect and colour of Sadhana. To read them is to get in contact with the Consciousness behind them. Take up any page from their writings. Do not try to understand in the way of a school-student. Read slowly a line, a paragraph and pause. You become aware of a wave of Peace somewhere, a current of joy somewhere. Read again, read ahead. Slowly the understanding will dawn and with it some crust fall broken, some contact be established. Have a fixed, regular hour for these studies which are best done alone and that too so long as there is no feeling of tiredness. The mind gets quieted, processed and readied to receive and enlarge itself into a greater Consciousness. Not only that. The Mother once observed that the mind grows in stature; at the best, new cells begin to form in the brain and a new receptacle is forged for the New Knowledge that is pressing to manifest.

Or you love the Divine, love Her who embodies for us the Divine — our adored Mother. Who can help loving Her? Brimming with compassion, supreme Love emanating from every pore of the body, there She stands the Light of our lights, the Life of our lives, bearing with all our foibles, bathing us incessantly in the streams of Her uplifting and transforming Consciousness. Even the worst among us has a corner which loves Her. You have known moments when you have melted in utter love for Her. Do not let that love dissipate itself. Gather all the threads of this love, raise their intensity by constant adoration, confirm them by ceaseless consecration in every detail of daily life, abandon yourself to Her outstretched arms with confidence. Loose yourself into Her and emerge as one wave of the Love that is the Mother.

Sadhana and Life

Your experiences of sensation in the chest, occasional movements in the *muladhara*, sound in the ears, slackening of memory, doubling of appetite and pressure of sleep are unmistakable signs and results of the working of the Yoga-shakti. Different systems react differently to this working. In your case, the pressure of the higher force has obviously touched the heart centre and set into movement the current of joy which derives initially from the emotional and more deeply from the Psychic being. The *muladhara* being the base of the *prana shakti*, it was inevitable that it responded by occasional stirrings. One of the first results of this inpour of the force is to awaken the aspiration all over the being. And aspiration is a movement towards infinity, towards expansion, enlargement. This usually is felt as a seeking for the higher light and consciousness in the mind, or, as an intense longing for the Divine in the heart. But it can also render itself physically in terms of hunger, as it has done in your case. But it will not be like that for all time. Another result of the yogic working in your being has been to push you inwards: the poise has shifted inside. That is why there is a tendency to sleep more, for in your present state of consciousness that is the only way of letting yourself live away from the surface.

So you see that you are already in the sadhana. There should be no conflict between your outer life as a school teacher and your inner life as a sadhak. The reconciliation lies in a sincere attempt to govern day to day activities, as far as possible and practicable, by the dictates of the growing Light within. That way you confirm in yourself all the time what you gain during special periods of inner sadhana.

I would suggest that you read and re-read the Mother's book *"Four Austerities and Four Liberations."*

Now to come to the general questions you have asked:

Question 1: *What is the connection between the Mother's Force and Kundalini Shakti?*

Answer: The Force that the Mother embodies and directs is what we may call the Cosmic Mahashakti. It is the Supreme Consciousness-Force that has brought out these worlds, sustains them and leads them to their destined goal. The Kundalini shakti — whether in the universe or in the individual — is only one formulation of this vast Divine Shakti. The Kundalini is primarily the *prana shakti* concerned with the organism in which it is housed. There are other formulations of Shakti on other levels like the mind, etc. In short, the Kundalini is subsidiary and subject to the rule of the infinitely greater and vaster Dynamism, i.e. the Mother's Force.

Question 2: *Are sadhaks hindered by the obstacles put forth by charms and spells cast by black-magic?*

Answer: It is a fact that normally these spells have their own effect on the intended victims. But if the individual is under the protective influence of a deity or guru, and he takes care to be always within this wall of protection, none of these things can touch him. And when the operation is so rendered ineffective, it goes back with a rebound and hits the source. Also if the person is a man of strong will and individuality, he cannot be imposed upon by anyone.

Question 3: *What is Occultism? And should a sadhak learn it to avert such dangers?*

Answer: Broadly speaking, Occultism is the knowledge and science of the control of the organisation of forces in

Nature that incessantly work behind the surfaces. It is a big subject and it is not safe to enter into it without the close guidance of an adept. However, there is no need for every sadhak to learn these things and use this knowledge if he develops a faith in the guru or the Divine of his ideal, relies upon it and takes care to be sincere to the inner vocation in his day to day life. Things are averted by the protective Influence without one's having to call for it.

Question 4: *How to cause the Psychic to come forward and lead the sadhana? Does fasting help here?*

Answer: By inner purification and aspiration. By purification I mean elimination of those movements from one's consciousness as have a veiling or obstructive effect on the soul within. Movements of disharmony, ugliness, anger, cruelty, animality come under this category. They not only soil the white purity of the Psychic within, but build a thick covering which is difficult for the rays of the Psychic to penetrate. Naturally, one has to aspire for this Antaratman to unveil himself and to emerge into overt operation. But it is much more necessary to create within oneself the climate where this emergence can take place, and, having taken place, maintain itself. A habitual turn towards cheerfulness, happiness, joy, sympathy, love, friendliness, a seeking for beauty and harmony in the movements within and without are some of the essential conditions for this purpose.

Bhakti, devotion, is a powerful factor to eliminate much obstructive impurity and create the environment that invites the Psychic influence.

Fasting has no place in this context. What fasting normally does is to create an artificial state of being in which the physical force is depressed and the vital energy assumes a greater role than normal. Consequently, there is a feeling of pleasurable excitement, a sense of power; but it is an unnatural state in which one can easily open to any kind of force benevolent or malevolent. The dangers of such a condition make it a risky and a wholly unnecessary venture.

Question 5: *How to know that one has a real call for Sri Aurobindo's Yoga?*

Answer: The central feature of Sri Aurobindo's Yoga which distinguishes it from other yogas is its insistence on a total transformation of human nature into the divine nature. If you have the urge to so change yourself, if you have the faith that it is possible for the Yoga-shakti to work out this transformation of human nature, and you feel a readiness to subject yourself to the inner discipline necessitated by this process, then you can be sure you are meant for this path.

Question 6: *Is it not undesirable to spend one's energy in academic courses instead of directing it towards sadhana? Does it not make one ambitious?*

Answer: Not necessarily. It depends upon the purpose for which one studies. If studies are undertaken to equip oneself by way of knowledge, cultivation of the mind and, generally, to one's enlightenment, then they are positive helps contributing to the growth of the general consciousness. Properly conducted with a wholesome background, studies can become a part of sadhana. The mental instrument gets used to exercising its faculties, tends to get subtilised and a way is prepared for the opening up of the higher reaches of the mind.

As for ambition, it is surely not confined to the academic sphere. Even an ignoramus can have — and usually does have — his own ambitions. Only, in the case of the educated, there is a possibility of the elimination of such perversions of aspiration with the increase of enlightenment.

After Death

Regarding your question about the relative roles of the psychic, the Self and the soul after death, and also which of them survives and what happens to the rest:

In the first place, it is necessary to have a clear conception of each of these terms: psychic, Self, soul.

The Self, Atman, stands aloof from manifestation. This Atman is indeed One. But in multiplicity It poises Itself as so many Jivatmans, Central Beings, presiding over their respective individual manifestations. I have said presiding; perhaps overseeing is more exact. The point is , the Jivatman, or the self of each individual, is not involved in the process of manifestation; it is not touched by birth and death. It is above them.

This Self, however, projects an emanation of Itself into the manifestation; this emanation or delegate is a spark of the Divine — the Self being Divine in its nature — and it passes through a series of births and deaths growing in experience and stature in the process: it evolves. This evolving entity is called the psychic being or the soul. Thus it is this psychic being at the centre that forms the core of the evolutionary movement of every individual life. What happens at death is that the physical body is first shed. Then the psychic being leaves in the subtle body consisting of the various sheaths of life, mind, etc., carrying with it the essence of all experience gathered during its life-time. After a period of transition in the intervening planes or worlds, it goes to the psychic world for rest, assimilation of the experience of the life left behind and preparation for the next birth.

Thus it is the psychic being that continues to be active even after death. In fact, it is the line from life to life giving continuity to the individual evolution. The Self is aloof in death as in birth: it watches and waits till the delegate it has sent forth grows and arrives at a stage and the spark grown into a flame below merges or joins the parent flame above. For all practical purposes the soul and the psychic being can be said to be the same. If a distinction is to be drawn between the two, it will be right to say that the soul involved in the manifestation and participating in the evolution is the psychic being. That is to say, a soul which does not participate in the evolution, but chooses to withdraw from the manifestation, cannot be called the psychic being.

The Kundalini Yoga and
The Integral Yoga

You refer to the Kundalini Yoga of the Tantras *vis-a-vis* the Integral Yoga of Sri Aurobindo. Indeed the principle is the same as far as the main process is concerned. The lower consciousness in Nature rises to meet and join the higher Consciousness; the higher descends and takes up the lower in itself. When this union is complete there is an inner liberation. Broadly, in the Tantras, the consciousness-energy in the body is led upwards through a sustained discipline — physical, psychophysical and psychological — step by step through the various nodal points in the subtler body till it reaches the highest point of the embodied Consciousness at the crown of the head. As you know, these points are not like physical points; they are pictured variously as chakras or lotuses etc. But they are not organs. They are the junctures where the various subtle nerve channels in their respective areas meet. Thus they function as focal points from which the fields governed by them can be acted upon. They do not have a substance different from the rest of the subtle body. There is naturally no question in the Tantras, of changing the "substance of the centres". To change the substance of the body is not part of the Tantric scheme. The centres come into the picture as passages to be opened by the pressure of the Yogic movement. You will recall that in the imagery of the Tantra, each centre is represented as a lotus with its petals hanging downward and when the ascending force strikes the lotus, it turns and blooms upward. And, in so doing, it provides the passage and its function is over at that moment. I mention all this to underline the fact that the centres or chakras in the Kundalini Yoga are mainly treated as gates of passage, the sole object of concentration being the Sahasrara which is the goal. It is only secondarily that the centres come to be concentrated upon for acting upon the principles, tattwas, of existence governed by them, for definite purposes.

In the Integral Yoga the principle of the joining of the lower terms of consciousness with the higher term obtains. But the process is not of ascent only. Helping the ascent, lifting it up is the higher consciousness which descends. The major part of the work is done by the descending Shakti and this Shakti chooses its own centres of action, the point at which it will touch and take into itself the aspiring human consciousness. It chooses its own order in keeping with the development of the individual. It does not follow a fixed order as in the other Yoga. Its action on the cells in the body is felt only in the later stages. The changing and rearrangement of the substance to which you refer also comes later and is done all over the being, not merely at the centres.

You ask if it is not true that among the centres the Ajna presents more difficulties than others. Not necessarily. It may be in some cases where the resistance is more on the mental level. After all, each centre is the acme, the high point of the forces active on the plane of being to which it belongs and its hardness or resistance is only a concentrated projection of the state of obscurity and inertia in that part. So it varies from person to person, where one finds it more easy or more difficult to negotiate.

You speak of "breaking" of the *knots*, and ask whether loosening is not better for our purpose. Actually, there is no breaking, no cutting asunder. What are called knots are just wrong twists in the placement of the subtle channels of consciousness within the system. Passage is either forced through them or negotiated through them, and, in the process they get disentangled. The physical feeling may be one of breaking, that is all.

Regarding the easiest and the safest way of the liberation of the knots and the change of centres, the right course for a sadhaka of the Integral Yoga is to leave the initiative in the hands of the Yoga-Shakti at work, trustfully, confining himself to the incessant task of perfecting his surrender to it in every part of the being, offering a pliable instrument, a ready field, to the Shakti to do what it wills. The Shakti knows what is to be done where and when. In any case, the work of transformation of the consciousness and its centres, the transmutation of the substance of the body cannot be done under the lead of the human intelligence in the shadow of Ignorance. It can be effected only by a Consciousness-Force that comes from a source transcendent of the field of its operation. Our part is to look up to it, enlarge ourselves, receive its impact without spilling and be vigilantly co-operative with its demands of receptivity, plasticity and sincerity.

OTHER TITLES BY SRI M.P. PANDIT

available from your local bookseller or

LOTUS LIGHT PUBLICATIONS
PO Box 1008
Silver Lake, WI 53170
414/889-8501

SRI AUROBINDO AND HIS YOGA

by M.P. Pandit

$6.95; 196 pp.; paper; ISBN: 0-941524-25-6

"Reacting to the importunities of biographers, Sri Aurobindo once remarked that none could write on his life for it was not there on the surface for man to see." Thus does Sri Pandit introduce the subject of this book; the life and work of the great, modern Indian Sage, Sri Aurobindo. Sri Aurobindo's life was one of spiritual realization, a life characterized by inner vision. The writings of Sri Aurobindo are a chronicle of that inner vision — multi-faceted, universal, always moving beyond established limits. The yoga of Sri Aurobindo "aims at the liberation and *perfection* of not any one part alone, but of the whole of the being of man." His Integral Yoga takes up all aspects of man, both inwardly and outwardly in his life in the world.

Sri Pandit gives us an overview of Sri Aurobindo's life, his writings and his integral yoga. In doing so he takes time to introduce the major practices of yoga and relates in a simple, yet dynamic, form the path open to the seeker of spiritual perfection.

WISDOM OF THE VEDA

M.P. PANDIT
$7.95 112 pp; paper
ISBN 0-941524-55-8

VEDIC DEITIES

M.P. PANDIT
$7.95 129 pp; paper
ISBN 0-941524-45-0
$7.95

GEMS FROM SRI AUROBINDO, 1st SERIES

Compiled by M.P. Pandit
$8.95; 133 pp; ISBN 0-941524-33-7.
Aphoristic thoughts and themes for
meditation on a wide range of subjects.

VEDIC SYMBOLISM

by Sri Aurobindo
compiled by Sri. M.P. Pandit

$6.95; 122 pp.; paper; ISBN: 0-941524-30-2

The value of the Rig Veda as a guidebook to spiritual
practice has been obscured due to the heavy veil of
symbols used by the Rishis to hide their meaning
from the uninitiated. Sri Aurobindo, through many
years of research and sadhana, was able to unlock the
secret of the veda and give us the key to the symbolic
system of the Vedic Rishis.

"Vedic Symbolism" introduces the major vedic concepts and reveals their esoteric sense.
Sri Aurobindo's work has given the study of the Rig Veda new relevance and has made the
imagery of the Veda reveal its hidden meaning. It is an important contribution to the vedic
literature.